# Marketing

## Tony Gray

*Series Editor*
*Susan Grant*
*West Oxfordshire College*

Heinemann

Heinemann Educational Publishers
Halley Court, Jordan Hill, Oxford OX2 8EJ
a division of Reed Educational & Professional Publishing Ltd

OXFORD   MELBOURNE   AUCKLAND
JOHANNESBURG   BLANTYRE   GABORONE
IBADAN   PORTSMOUTH (NH) USA   CHICAGO

Heinemann is a registered trademark of Reed Educational & Professional Publishing Ltd

Text © Tony Gray, 2000
First published in 2000

04 03 02 01 00
9 8 7 6 5 4 3 2 1

All rights reserved.

**British Library Cataloguing in Publication Data**
A catalogue record for this book is available from the British Library

ISBN 0 435 330 497

Typeset and illustrated by Wyvern 21 Ltd, Bristol

Printed and bound in Great Britain by Biddles Ltd, Guildford

**Author Acknowledgements**
The author would like to thank Annabel, Nicholas Kehoe, Robert Bircher, Mick Watson, Sophie Williams, Sue Walton, and above all, Susan Grant, for their considerable assistance.

**Acknowledgements**
The publishers would like to thank the following for permission to reproduce copyright material: AQA for the AEB and AQA examination questions used in this book; *The Daily Telegragph* for the extract on p.95; *The Financial Times* for the extract on p.121; *The Guardian* for the extracts by J. Crace on pages 2 and 12, the extract by R. Reeves on p.9, the extract by J. Dunn on p.22, the extract by M. Bunting on p.27, the extract by L. Proddow on p.39, the extract by R. Howell on p.49, the extract by J. Finch on p. 56, the graph by C. Barrie on p.76, the extract on p.87, the extract on p.102, the extract by I. Darby on p.110, and the extract by J. McCellan on p.117; Hodder and Stoughton for the figure on p.41; *The Independent* for the material on p.50; *Marketing* for the extract on p.108; *The Observer* for the Figure on p.16, the cartoon on p.81 and the extract on p.98; Prentice Hall for the graph on p.18.
The publishers have made every effort to contact copyright holders. However, if any material has been incorrectly acknowledged, the publishers would be pleased to correct this at the earliest opportunity

Tel: 01865 888058 www.heinemann.co.uk

# Contents

| | | |
|---|---|---|
| *Preface* | | *iv* |
| *Introduction* | | 1 |
| *Chapter One* | Marketing principles | 2 |
| *Chapter Two* | Marketing plan | 11 |
| *Chapter Three* | Marketing strategy | 23 |
| *Chapter Four* | Market research | 40 |
| *Chapter Five* | Product | 53 |
| *Chapter Six* | Price | 65 |
| *Chapter Seven* | Place | 77 |
| *Chapter Eight* | Promotion campaigns | 88 |
| *Chapter Nine* | Promotional methods | 97 |
| *Chapter Ten* | Development in marketing: Relationship, e-commerce and international | 112 |
| *Conclusion* | | 122 |
| *Index* | | 123 |

# Preface

Marketing is a key topic on the new AS/A level specifications, GNVQ, HND and University Business Studies courses. This is, of course, because of its crucial role in determining the success of companies.

In this book Tony Gray explores the nature, functions, methods and performance of marketing and examines recent developments in marketing. The book's particular strengths lie in the wide range of real world examples it includes and its coverage of how the internet is changing the world of marketing.

Tony Gray is Head of Economics and Politics and Deputy Head of Business and Vocational Studies at Cardinal Vaughan Memorial School. He is an experienced teacher of marketing and has practical experience gained from working for the Institute for Public Policy Research and for Baptie and Co., one of Europe's leading direct and channel marketing companies.

Susan Grant
*Series Editor*

# Introduction

What this book aims to do is to provide the reader with a concise overview of marketing and the developments which are changing the world of marketing at the dawn of the new millennium. For the UK the biggest changes are access to the European and Net market which this book places a heavy emphasis on throughout.

How a business or organization goes about marketing its assets decides whether it dies or thrives. *Chapter One* introduces some of the key principles and terms used in marketing, and provides a background guide to marketing.

It is often said in the marketing world that a well-executed marketing plan is a thing of beauty. *Chapter Two* covers what a basic marketing plan is, and methods used to put it together, implement and appraise.

*Chapter Three* explains what marketing strategy is and how it differs from the corporate strategy. Special emphasis is placed on how attempts have been made to carve out an unbeatable niche in the marketplace – the Unique Selling Point.

The importance of market research and different methods of research are examined in *Chapter Four*.

*Chapter Five* looks at the key characteristics of a product, how it fits into a product range, alternative product life cycles (PLCs), positioning, packaging, new product development and the different methods of branding that are used.

*Chapter Six* examines how to ensure that the 'price is right'. Price determination, price strategies and price discrimination are discussed.

Place, covered in *Chapter Seven*, is more than just being shopper friendly with good layouts and displays. It is also concerned with 'distribution channel marketing.' The types of intermediaries (so called middle-men), retailers, and transportation are discussed.

*Chapter Eight* introduces planning a promotional mix campaign with the application of AIDA, DAGMAR, push and pull promotional strategies, and the influences behind any promotional campaign such as ANSOFF, PEST and Product Life Cycles.

*Chapter Nine* explores above and below line promotional methods. It looks at the different mediums in the UK and Europe used to advertise and the latest UK and European legal restrictions on promotions.

*Chapter Ten* expands on the latest developments in marketing. It explores the revolutionary impact the Net and globalization are having in the world of marketing, discussing the rise of relationship marketing, mass customization and the death of the middleman.

## Chapter One

# Marketing principles

*'Marketing is the art of making someone want something you have.'*
The Internet Nonprofit Center

---

## What is marketing?

**Marketing** is about selling by promoting the right product, at the right price in the right place. This can be summarized by planning and executing the right **marketing mix**, which covers the four Ps of product, price, place and promotion.

The key to marketing is about winning and keeping customers, and it is therefore 'the art of gentle seduction'. It involves using instincts, hard negotiations and emotions. Companies like Go (a subsidiary of British Airways offering cheap flights) and Tesco have found that a firm commitment to marketing reaps profits, by placing the customers **needs and wants** at the centre of their organization.

*'Because its purpose is to create a customer, the business has two and only two functions: marketing and innovation. Marketing and innovation create value, all the rest are costs.'*
P Drucker, *People and Performance*, Harper College Press, 1977

This means that even for organizations where profit is not the prime objective marketing remains essential.

---

### Marketing - an exact science

JOHN CRACE

You wander into a supermarket. Your eyes lazily scan the shelves before you select a few items and bung them in your trolley. If you could be bothered to think about it in any depth, you'd probably come to the conclusion that your weekly shop was a small expression of freewill; but as you can't, it's just an annoyingly mindless chore.

To a marketer, though, you'd be wrong on both counts. There's no freewill or mindlessness attached to shopping, only an illusion of them. A customer doesn't buy something; he or she is sold it, either by direct or subliminal messages. So when you pick out a particular soap powder from the countless varieties on offer you are responding either to an advert, word of mouth, packaging or shelf position. Whatever it is that finally sways you, it is another victory for the marketers.

Extract from 'Battle of the brands' in the *Guardian*, September 14, 1999

---

## Defining the market

Most decisions on what to produce, how to produce, where to produce and for whom to produce take place in the market place. A market occurs whenever consumers make contact with sellers to satisfy their 'needs or wants'. By its very nature a market does not have to be a physical place but can take place on the telephone or increasingly on the Internet. Examples of markets include the consumer goods market, capital goods market, the financial market, the property market, labour market and the market in services such as leisure and tourism.

## Meeting needs and wants

Marketing seeks to meet **needs and wants**. Basic needs are those required for physical survival i.e. food, shelter, warmth and water. According to Abraham Maslow (*Motivation and Personality*, 1954) there is a hierarchy of needs, as shown in Figure 1, which explains why people are driven by particular needs at different times from the most to the least pressing:

Needs can also be social in the sense of people needing to feel secure and belonging to a society, or individual in terms of education and the freedom of self-expression. Wants tend to be for those goods and services that are desired but not required for survival. They tend to be shaped by the culture a person lives in and their individual personality. The difference between wants and needs is not always clear-cut as often a want is also about satisfying a need.

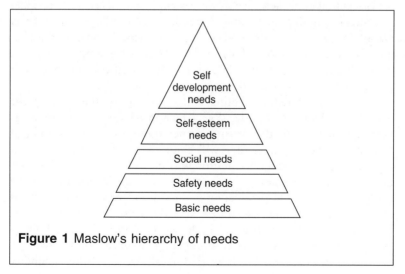

**Figure 1** Maslow's hierarchy of needs

## Maslow's pyramid toppled

To many in marketing Maslow's hierarchy of needs has been toppled. This is a result of the demise of social classifications (despite increased inequality) and the supremacy of universal non hierarchical needs, instead of the old hierarchy based on aspirations. For example, the poorest in society have other needs than survival; and designer products whether Gucci clothes or Stella lager are no longer niche luxury brands but offer prestige to their owners. According to John Grant, (New Marketing Manifesto, 1999, Orion) Maslow's hierarchy has been replaced by fifteen fundamental human drives. Amongst the fifteen drives are: the 'sex drive' tapped by Häagen Dazs ice cream; 'hunger' being more about dieting and gourmet foods than survival; and 'curiosity' with Microsoft encouraging people to 'surf the net.'

## A brief history of marketing

The history of marketing is vague with no agreed periods or dates. What is apparent is that different marketing concepts have dominated in different periods, so that marketing 'eras' can be identified.

### The production era

Marketing today is very different to that of a century ago. When Henry Ford first sold his Model T in 1908 he famously offered 'any colour you like . . . as long as it's black,' because black was the quickest drying paint and therefore the easiest to mass produce. This **product orientated** approach focuses on designing and making the product and then promoting the completed product. Its dominance in the early twentieth century has resulted in this time being known as the production era. Silent movie fans in the 1920s, for example, were not demanding talking pictures. The idea is that often consumers do not know what they want until it is set before them.

Product orientated marketing still exists, as in the case of the Millennium Dome or London Eye. The approach with the latter has been a fulfilment of the Kevin Costner quote in the film 'Field of Dreams': 'If you build it they will come.' One of the least successful examples of product orientation was the Sinclair C5 mobile computerized cart; sales never took off, as there was no demand for the product. However, a product orientated good can be successful if carefully designed and promoted, like the Dyson vacuum cleaner, for example. Often market research will be undertaken on how to best promote the completed product. The disadvantage with a product-orientated approach is that it allows for little flexibility for individuals or segments as it puts the product before the market.

## The sales era

As the mid-twentieth century generated a greater number of products in response to increasing population sizes and competition, marketing entered a sales era where companies had to spend more time and money marketing their products. This mainly took the form of **product-variety marketing,** still used today, which emphasizes a variation on the standard product in terms of different features, styles, quality and sizes. For example, as tastes changed over time so did Coca Cola by producing Cherry Coke, different soft drinks, and differently sized containers from mini-cans to multi-packs.

## Mass marketing

During most of the twentieth century mass production and mass consumption was met with **mass marketing,** mass distribution and mass promotion promoting one product to the mass society. Mass marketing that dominated the production and sales era was aspirational, a case of keeping up with the Joneses. Mass marketing today concerns the selling of the largest volume of the same product at the lowest cost and price to the largest potential market; as is the case with most fast moving consumer goods (**FMCGs**) like soap powders, food or other groceries.

## The marketing era

The marketing era, in which we currently live, has been dominated by **market orientated** products, which identify market segments and are tailored to meet needs. For example, non caffeine diet Coca-Cola appeals to the more health conscious who still want to drink Coke.

With market orientated products, the focus is on undertaking market research to see what the consumer wants and then making the good or service to meet their requirements. This is the approach that has been adopted with Sony Playstation II responding to customer demands. Time and effort spent on market research may enable the firm to be flexible and adaptable to the demands of the market thereby increasing its chances of success and survival:

*'Figure out what is desirable and make that what you deliver; or figure out what you can deliver and make that desirable. But remember, the former is a lot easier than the latter.'*

Sergio Zyman, Coca-Cola's former Chief Marketing Officer, *The End of Marketing As We Know It,* Harper Collins, 1999

Market orientated products require:

- market positioning – finding a competitive position and suitable marketing mix;
- market **segmentation** – each segment has separate product and marketing mixes;
- market targeting – evaluating and selecting attractive segments to enter.

## Market segments

A market segment is a set of buyers who share common needs or characteristics. Market segments are only useful if they help target customers. How to evaluate, select and target segments is a complicated process.

To be useful and effective to marketing, market segments must be:

- Measurable – the size and characteristics of groups might be difficult to measure; for example how do you measure someone's personality?
- Accessible – some groups are difficult to reach with marketing and distribution activities, for example night-shift workers.
- Substantial – being profitable or the largest possible homogenous group.
- Actionable – depending on the ability of the company to serve and attract the segment.

Within the marketing concept, various types of segmentation can be used to target most successfully the existing or potential customer. The different segments include:

- *Geographic* segments split the market into target sales regions or by country.
- *Demographic* measures split the market according to age, gender, family size, education, occupation, income, religion or culture. Market research companies like Mintel uses life stages: Pre-Family under 35 year olds with no dependants; Empty-Nesters aged 35–54 with no family; Family Nesters under 54 year olds with children under 15 year olds living at home; and Post Family over 55 year olds.
- *Psychographic* includes the main measure of 'social class', personality types or life-style categorizations. For example, the Institute of Grocery Distribution, an independent research organization, classifies their consumers using 'life-style' categories as:

'Anarchists' who never cook for themselves and eat what they want when they want; 'Time Valuers' who are younger working people without dependants who eat one main meal a day and snack; 'Traditionalists' who take two main meals a day plus nibbles; and 'Sensibles' who eat a nutritious balanced diet.

- *Behaviouristic* segments can cover a wide range of variables. These variables include: 'purchase' occasion such as birthdays or weddings, the use the product is put to, and the benefits sought by the consumer. Other factors to consider are the user's status from non-user to habitual repeat business; the usage rate measuring the frequency of purchases, and loyalty status identifying brand loyalist or brand switchers. The attitude of the consumer will also have an impact on their behaviour; a bad experience may lead to a negative attitude towards the product. The stage of readiness (**AIDA**) of the consumer can also be used. AIDA stands for the segments of the market who are: aware the product exists; show interest in the product; *desire* the product; and those who are actually prepared to take action by buying the product.

  Customer behaviour can also be used to segment the market based on how the decision to buy is made from the *initiator* to the user. The initiator is the person who first thinks about buying; in the case of children this is known as '**pester power**' as with Alton Towers or Sunny Delight. The *influencer* is the person whose advice carries the most weight. The *decider* is the person who decides to buy. The *buyer* is the one who makes the actual purchase and finally there is the *user* of the bought product.

## Socio-Economic Groups (SEGs) or Social Class

### The ABC1 system
The most common form of market segmentation used in the market orientated approach was the ABC1 social classification system, which was conceived in the 1930s and came to prominence in the 1950s.

Socio-economically society is divided into segments according to social class and income level, traditionally this took the form of: A, B, C1, C2, D and E segments:

|   |   |
|---|---|
| A | Higher managerial and professionals |
| B | Intermediate managerial, administrative and professional |
| C1 | Supervisory, clerical, junior administrative or professional |
| C2 | Skilled manual |
| D | Semi-skilled and unskilled manual |
| E | State pensioners, widows, casual and lowest grade earners. |

The ABC1 system, used by the Government and adopted by many market research firms, assumes that spending habits and consumer attitudes can be split into six categories based on social grade. The social class and grading were occupation-based as society was assumed to follow a hierarchy based on employment and income. This has increasingly been viewed as out of date and often difficult to judge as people have become increasingly occupationally mobile.

### The Newly Revised Social Class System

A new method of market segmentation, based on socio-economic groupings from 1 to 7, has been introduced for the 2001 National Census. The Newly Revised Social Class System measures employment relationships between the manager and the managed, as well as the job security and autonomy people have at work (i.e. the ability to be your own boss).

## Market segmentation map

A market segmentation map is a useful tool for analysing the market and identifying gaps in the market that a market orientated approach can fill. Different sets of data can be brought together and overlaid. To enable firms, especially those in niche markets, to target those customers which are of greatest interest to them. These are known as *geodemographic* databases because they match an area against demographic profiles, such as income or age.

The most common geodemographic database used in marketing is **ACORN** (A Classification of Residential Neighbourhoods), which identifies key clusters of the population where people are likely to have similar lifestyles and purchasing habits. Data from the National Census ACORN can be used to target any geographical area from the national picture down to a neighbourhood of around 150 households. By covering every household using the Electoral Register, market research companies like CACI provide a customer profile for their clients which 'can select by surname or first name, or select neighbours to existing customers.' For example, CACI were able to provide a direct mail list of the best prospective customers for Woolwich Independent Financial Advisory Services, by matching present customer characteristics against ACORN data to find them.

## Micro/niche marketing

As the marketing era has developed markets have fragmented into smaller markets in response to more consumer power and greater competition. Market segments are increasingly seen as too broad based and are being split into micro or niche markets where tailored marketing programmes, known as **micro or niche marketing**, meet needs and wants in narrowly defined segments. An ironic twist on Henry Ford's Model T marketing slogan was the release in 1999 of a limited edition of 1,000 Ford Ka Black because black is now marketed as a luxury colour.

---

### I am not a number

RICHARD REEVES

'The millennium is acting as a kind of collective mid-life crisis. People are thinking "God, it'll be a new century, I can't think and act in the same way." More people are trying to figure out who they are'.

McKie's report, Tribes, commercially driven and prepared for Barclays Life, describes the new 'tribes' emerging in Britain, based on survey evidence and focus groups – the factory floor of the booming labelling industry.

The tribes range from Nomadic Networkers, living and working on the move using high-tech equipment; Barbie Babes, who live by their looks; Elders, who are poor but wise; to Villagers who recreate idealised community life around a welcoming supermarket.

One of the difficulties for the army of social analysts is that one of the strongest social trends of the past 30 years is the desire not to be pigeon-holed.

'In the past we could put people in boxes and pretty much rely on them to stay put,' McKie says. 'Now the social classification is more like a solar system, with people rotating around each other at different times. Someone may be part of one tribe during the day, and another altogether at night. It is shifting all the time.'

Extract from 'Marketing makes tribes of us all', *Guardian*, 18 July 1999

---

## The next marketing era

The ultimate fragmentation is customized marketing which targets specific customer or buyer organizations and relies on high standards in customer care. Complete market segmentation meeting customer needs as individuals, instead of broad classes or buyers, is known as **customization.**

Technological advances and the ability to sell on the Net has resulted in further developments in customized marketing, with the ability to meet individual requirements on a larger scale. For example, Dell computers prides itself on building computers to customer requirements. The customized era is most likely to dominate the twenty-first century.

---

### KEY WORDS

| | |
|---|---|
| Marketing | Market orientated |
| Marketing mix | Segmentation |
| Needs and wants | AIDA |
| Product orientated | Pester power |
| Product-variety marketing | ACORN |
| Mass marketing | Micro or niche marketing |
| FMCGs | Customization |

---

## Further reading

Grant, J., Part 1 in *The New Marketing Manifesto*, Orion, 1999.
Dibb, S. *et al.*, Chapter 1 in *Marketing*, Houghton & Mifflin, 1997.
Hall, D., Jones, R.and Raffo, C., Unit 36 in *Business Studies*, Causeway Press, 1999
Nowacki, J., *Business Resource Pack: Marketing*, Philip Allan, 1998.

## Useful websites

The on-line community for marketing: www.mad.co.uk
Introduction to marketing: www3.mistral.co.uk/jonmatt

## Essay topics

1. (a) Distinguish between product and market orientated products. [10 marks]
   (b) Explain the benefits to be obtained from using a market orientated approach. [15 marks]
2. (a) How can the work of a sociologist who studies human behaviour help a marketer? [10 marks]
   (b) 'In marketing terms Britain is now a classless society' Discuss. [15 marks]

## Chapter Two

# Marketing plan and implementation

*'Plan the sale when you plan the ad.'*
Leo Burnett

## The marketing plan

A **marketing plan** is a detailed, written document that sets out how a marketing campaign can be implemented, explaining the who, where, when and how. The marketing plan should explain where you are, where you are going and how you are going to get there. Marketing plans need to be updated over time usually on an annual basis and will, where necessary, vary along geographical, product or segment lines. The shape a marketing plan takes will depend on whether the marketing strategy is market or product orientated, but in either case the marketing plan should contain:

- mission statement
- executive summary
- business environment
- objectives
- strategy
- implementation – mix and tactics
- budget
- evaluation and controls

### Mission Statement

The **Mission statement** embodies the vision and values of a company, so that everyone knows what they are aiming for. For IKEA their mission statement is: 'To improve the everyday life of the majority of people.' For Adidas it is 'to be the best sports brand in the world.' The mission statement is important for the staff to motivate them and for consumers to fit the mission to their idea of what they are purchasing. From the overall priority contained in the mission statement, priorities for the marketing plan and strategic objectives can be established.

### Executive summary

The executive summary identifies the main objectives and

## Chartered Institute of Marketing (CIM) guide to the marketing plan

JOHN CRACE

One definition of marketing that is often given is that it is a 'management process responsible for identifying, anticipating and satisfying customer requirements profitably'.

In short, says Clare Thorpe, a spokesperson for CIM, 'the essence of marketing is customers. If you don't understand your customers you're not going to stay in business'. The first task of any marketing plan, then, is to identify potential customers and find out exactly what they want and how much they are prepared to pay for it. This can be done in a variety of ways, from New Labour-style focus groups to statistical market research.

Once a gap in the market has been identified, the next step is to create strategic objectives. 'These must be both achievable and measurable,' continues Thorpe. 'You have to know precisely what it is you are trying to do, be it increasing market awareness or share by 10% in the first year.

'When this has been decided you then look at the different forms of advertising media, such as direct mail, advertising, PR and the internet before developing the appropriate style of campaign. Chief executives, for example, respond to entirely different messages to those aimed at an 18 year old. The bottom line of any campaign is that you must be able to evaluate it. If it works, you must know why and if it doesn't, you must know why not.'

Extract from 'Battle of the brands' in the *Guardian*, 14 September 1999

recommendations. It contains a table of contents and enables the reader to understand the main points covered in the marketing plan.

### Business environment

The marketing plan will need to provide an analysis of the current marketing situation. John Harvey-Jones once said:

*'There is no point in deciding where your business is going until you have actually decided with great clarity where you are now.'*

Analysis uses **PEST** and **SWOT** to help to review the position of a product in the market.

## PEST

PEST or STEP factors summarize the external environment into:

Political laws and regulations which will affect the ability of businesses to market their products and to enter or leave markets.

Economic changes which will influence economic activity and business prospects. Changes in wages, inflation, interest rates, unemployment, government expenditure and taxation will all have an impact on the business environment.

Social and cultural changes which will alter a plan. For example, changes in the lifestyle of men and women in relationships, like the concept of the 'new man' identity, will have an impact on a product's image and promotion.

Technological developments for Microsoft originally meant a product orientated development of Basic as a language for computers. Then in 1983 Microsoft developed Windows as a universal operating environment for PCs, thus becoming more market orientated. Another example is the Internet book company Amazon which obtained a patent for the use of technology for '1-Click Ordering' that enables orders and payment to be processed online at the click of a button.

## Competition

An alternative to PEST is **LE PEST C** meaning Legal, Ecological, PEST and Competition.

Latent or new competitors might take a market by surprise and wipe out the business concerned. As a result understanding their competitor's objectives, strategy, resources customers, suppliers, finances and marketing mix is vital to the marketing strategy of a firm. The firm's objectives will provide clues to their strategy and marketing mix and will highlight where they might be vulnerable and how they are likely to react to competition.

Using consumer research the strengths and weaknesses of competitors can be identified. On this basis the firm can select competitors to attack and avoid. If their competitors are strong or even weak then little is to be gained from attacking, unless there is a greater return if they succeed in the long-term. Companies which are similar in competitive strength, whether located close or distant, can be effectively competed against.

Competition can come in different forms and firms need to be sure who their real competition is:

- Similar specific – when firms produce the same product with similar technology in the same market for example Nintendo 64 Dolphin, Sony 'Playstation 2' and Sega 'Dreamcast'.
- Similar general – when firms produce the same product but serve different market segments such as geographical or satisfying different needs which most food products do by offering varying levels of quality for the same product as in the case of vintage wine against 'cheap plonk'.
- Different specific – when the same need is satisfied by different

means for example Eurostar versus British Airways between London and Paris.

- Different general – this is when firms compete for discretionary expenditure, for example consumers use their discretion whether to buy a holiday or a new car.

The internal business environment also needs to be reviewed in terms of sales, price, gross profit margins, competition, stage in the product life cycle, promotion and distribution channels from producer to sales point specifying target markets.

## SWOT

SWOT analysis will look at the *strengths* of the product, for example, a perceived niche in the market, and *weaknesses* such as low sales. It will also anticipate *opportunities* such as markets where a competitive advantage can be gained; and anticipating *threats* such as potential competitor activities. Microsoft constantly undertakes SWOT analyses looking at its:

- Strengths in terms of product innovation, customer satisfaction and the quality of the workforce.
- Weaknesses keeping up with the pace of developments by constantly developing.
- Opportunities to deliver its vision of 'information at your fingertips'.
- Threats of further legal action and of the possible failure of complementary technology to keep up to pace with Microsoft.

## Objectives

There are a large number of potential objectives any firm can choose from for their marketing strategy. Careful analysis will be required to decide which is the most suitable. For newly established firms the first priorities are usually *entry* into an existing or new market and the establishment of the product. This will also be true for firms already established in a different market entering a new market, for example, Virgin Cola entering the cola market. For a small firm *survival* or maintaining the status quo might be the main strategy. For other firms being able to maintain their position in a shrinking market or as a niche operator might be the main objective.

Beyond entry and survival, *growth* will be the main objective of many firms. Growth however does not come without its risks in terms of resources and time. An attempt to grow too quickly can lead to a firm being over-stretched. This was the case in the 1980s as firms like the book store Dillons (now bought out by Waterstones) opened new stores rapidly and then when economic activity declined the firm was stuck with too many outlets with high rents.

Growth can be measured in different ways, depending on the general objective of growth in the market. For most businesses growth will mean maximising profit. A target for profit is set, which is sales revenue minus costs. **Profitability** as an objective might not be associated with growth if a firm is seeking to make a short-term profit by getting the best return for a product that is declining, known as *harvesting* or *milking*, by using minimum promotional expenditure. Although it is generally assumed that most firms will be profit maximizers, for some the objective will be to maximize *turnover* by setting a target for sales from which revenue will be received.

Other objectives in terms of growth can be about maximising *market size* in terms of the value of sales in the market. This is measured by the value of sales or the number of units sold. In terms of competitors, taking a larger **market share** as a percentage of all the sales in the market will be the key growth objective. Market share can be measured by the value of sales or number of units sold. In the European beer market the main brewing firms are competing in terms of defeating competitors by getting the largest market share as illustrated in Figure 2. If the organization is in the non-profit sector other objectives will be prioritized. For example, for a school the quality of education measured by results, or for a political party electoral victory. Firms might adopt social-environmental objectives using 'cause-related marketing' (**CRM**) to promote good causes and project the brand as more caring and community focused. An example would be Iceland's link with the National Missing Persons Helpline. Cause related marketing can go wrong if the consumers view it as a cynical marketing ploy to boost sales, as in the case of Flora's promotion using Princess Diana's signature, which was criticized for being in bad taste.

In trying to meet these objectives different factors will need to be taken into account. The objective will need to match the viewpoint of sellers, buyers, legislators, competitors and other groups if it is to succeed. If it does not the first objective will be to change the perceptions of different groups. The firm will maximize its chances of achieving the objective if the society in which it operates is orientated towards that objective be it maximising consumption, consumer satisfaction, choice, or quality of life.

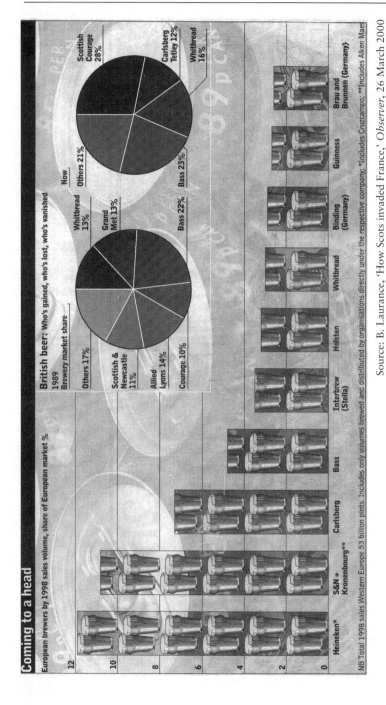

Source: B. Laurance, 'How Scots invaded France,' *Observer*, 26 March 2000

**Figure 2** Market shares in the European beer market

## Strategy

In order to deliver its objectives, a firm will decide on a **marketing strategy** (as covered in Chapter Three) and must make a strategic use of the **marketing mix,** known as the four Ps: 'product, price, place and promotion.'

- **Product** (covered in Chapter Five) defines the characteristics of the product to meet customer requirements, and includes packaging and branding to add value.
- **Price** (covered in Chapter Six) concerns the pricing strategy to be adopted in determining the price; even offering the product for free is a pricing strategy.
- **Place** (covered in Chapter Seven), also known as distribution, looks at the location and delivery of a product.
- **Promotion** (covered in Chapters Eight and Nine) includes channel marketing using media to advertise, direct marketing which is one-to-one selling using sales personnel, direct-mail or tele-sales; public relations; and sales promotions, for example, special offers.

## Implementation

An action programme for **implementation** as part of the marketing plan is essential. This explains how the plan can be implemented, what to do, when to do it, and how much it will cost covering, for example, media types and time-tabling promotional offers.

Implementation is a key part of the plan: too often a marketing plan can be poorly implemented. To overcome this the marketing plan must ensure that long-term and short-term objectives are carefully balanced. Otherwise most people implementing the plan will be tempted to meet short-term objectives and lose sight of the long-term objectives for which they feel they will only be rewarded in the future.

Implementation plans must also allow for flexibility as internal and external factors can change, making a less flexible plan quickly outdated and irrelevant. Other problems to be overcome are how the marketing plan is to be received by those implementing the plan. A lack of specificity in spelling out the detail can lead to confusion. A poorly communicated plan to the sales-force and others will result in them continuing to carry out other activities irrespective of the plan. These communication problems can stem from an inability to inform or persuade. The latter will lead to inertia as sales-staff might be resistant to change and stick to habits which the marketing plan might have identified as no longer working. It is therefore important for a sales force to share the vision espoused in the plan. Finally, the marketing plan might have to overcome the organizational structure of the firm to ensure successful implementation. With central hierarchical planning or top-down management it is difficult to co-ordinate and manage problems with agents in the market often remaining isolated from the marketing plan.

## The marketing budget

The marketing **budget** for the plan can be developed using a number of methods. Target profit planning estimates the marketing budget from the target profit, which is calculated by subtracting the expected total costs from the expected total sales revenue. Alternatively 'profit optimization planning' can be used. This identifies the relationship between sales and the amount spent on marketing. As illustrated in Figure 3, the marketing budget should come between the net profit range $M^0$-$M^1$ and is optimized at $M^x$.

The sales revenue curve is S shaped as low marketing expenditure will have little impact on sales, whilst an increase in marketing expenditure will suddenly result in a pick up in sales. Eventually sales revenue will flatten and decrease as diminishing returns from high levels of marketing expenditure occur due to increased competition and sales resistance. By taking away total costs, including marketing expenditure, a net profit is derived from which a percentage can be committed to the marketing budget.

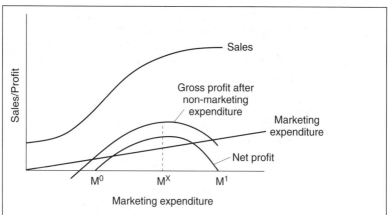

**Figure 3** The marketing budget (Source: Principles of Marketing, P. Kotler and G. Armstrong, Prentice-Hall 1991)

Estimating sales revenue is a difficult if often inaccurate process. The three most common methods used are statistical, experimental and judgmental. Statistical methods use past data and have the danger of the marketing budget looking in the rear-view mirror rather than the potential market ahead. Experimental methods try to overcome this by using pilots varying the promotional mix and noting the response. The judgmental method is about making intelligent guesses about the likely responses to changes in the marketing budget.

## Evaluation and control

Management control is required to measure and for **evaluation** of progress with the implementation of the plan and to take corrective action. During the year checks can be made on performance in sales, expenses, and customer attitudes against the plan. Errors can be corrected by top management action. The *profitability* of the company will act as a **control** as it will indicate if the plan is being successfully implemented and highlight potential problems. Market line managers can determine profitability using profit and loss statements of different products, identifying where the company is making a profit or a loss for example as a result of expensive rent or transportation. The firm can also use *strategic controls* using the market audit to determine the overall effectiveness of the marketing plan, which can quickly go out of date.

## A word of warning

Markets are dynamic and a firm that spends too much time putting together and implementing their market plan can be swept away by events or miss an opportunity.

## Market audit

A **market audit** is a comprehensive, systematic, independent, periodic examination of the company's environment, objectives, strategies and activities to determine the SWOT analysis of the firm and recommend a plan of action. The audit covers all marketing areas periodically. The auditor has the freedom to provide information which might surprise or shock the client, and can advise the client to pursue the best marketing opportunities and to do so efficiently.

A full market audit is a comprehensive document, which usually has six main sections:

1. Environment – this can be either macro or micro environment. The macro-environment concerns PEST and includes variations in the

natural environment such as pollution and demographic change. The micro level or the task environment is concerned with markets, customers, competitors, distributors and dealers, suppliers, marketing service firms and the different publics.

2. Strategy – this includes the mission statement, and strategy to meet the objectives and goals.

3. Organization – covers the optimal structure, control over activities, efficiency in communication, product management, training, and inter-department efficiency.

4. Systems – how information is gathered, effective planning and forecasts, whether effective control mechanisms are being regularly monitored, and how effective is new product development.

5. Productivity – the profitability of the range of products in the market, their cost effectiveness, and whether or not it is possible to reduce costs and increase productivity.

6. Mix – covers the product range, scope for new product development, price strategies, place and promotions.

Central to the market audit is the market research.

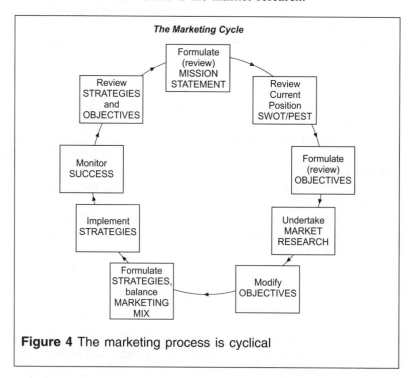

**Figure 4** The marketing process is cyclical

---

```
                        KEY WORDS
Marketing plan              Price
Mission statement           Place
PEST                        Promotion
SWOT                        CRM
LE PEST C                   Implementation
Profitability               Budget
Market size                 Evaluation
Market share                Controls
Marketing strategy          Market audit
Marketing mix               Marketing cycle
Product
```

## Marketing cycle

A marketing plan follows a **marketing cycle**: a continuous process of implementation, research and change, as illustrated in Figure 4.

## Further reading

Cohen, W. A., *The Marketing Plan*, John Wiley & Sons, 1998.

Jay, R., *Successful Marketing Plans in a week*, Hodder & Stoughton, 1999.

Kotler, P., Chapter 9 in *Kotler on Marketing*, Simon & Schuster, 1999.

Tinneswood, P., Chaper 12 in *Marketing and Production Decisions*, Longman, 1991.

## Useful websites

Browse through dozens of successful business plans: www.Bplans.com

Company annual reports on-line: www.carol.co.uk

## Essay topics

1. (a) Explain the different marketing objectives a firm might have? [12 marks]
   (b) Discuss the importance of market audits to the marketing of fast moving consumer goods. [13 marks]
2. (a) 'Effective marketing is the result of a quality marketing plan'. Discuss. [15 marks]
   (b) Identify the main features of a marketing plan. [10 marks]

## Data response question

Read the extract below from an article (by John Dunn) which appeared in the *Guardian* on 8 June 1999 and then answer the questions that follow.

### Do your homework, French professor tells small firms

Small firms rarely find enough time to stop and think about where they are going. Even when they pay to get expert marketing advice from Professor Paul Millier, head of industrial marketing at Lyon Business School in France, he says they still do not do their homework.

'They never sit down for even half an hour to reflect on their situation. When I work with them and tell them to write a marketing plan, they never do it. They are too busy.'

It may seem a paradox, he says, but small firms face exactly the same problems as big ones in getting innovations accepted. 'All companies have to convince someone. In big companies, the laboratory researcher has to convince his small business unit or marketing department. The entrepreneur has to convince his bank manager or his shareholders.'

'Carrying out a proper marketing study is a very good way of persuading them. But with small companies it's always the same. A year or two after they have started they have got a list of perhaps one or two hundred contacts they have made, but they don't have a proper view of their market.'

As a result, Mr Millier says, they spread their energy and resources over hundreds of clients rather than concentrating on a few market niches which are likely to prove successful. 'When you are a small firm you are always very busy. You are more comfortable taking the car to visit a client or picking up the phone to arrange an appointment, rather than stopping to reflect on your marketing strategy.'

1. 'When I work with them and tell them to write a marketing plan, they never do it. They are too busy.' Discuss the consequences of this statement. [8 marks]
2. How might the marketing plan of a small business be (i) similar to and (ii) differ from that of a large business? [6 marks]
3. How does the marketing strategy fit into the marketing plan? [5 marks]
4. Why are marketing plans used? [6 marks]

*Chapter Three*

# Marketing strategy

*'Strategy is the one thing that will keep you clean. When in doubt, just check whatever you want to do against strategy.'*
Sergio Zyman, Coca-Cola's former Chief Marketing Officer, in *The End of Marketing as we Know It*, Harper Collins, 1999

A marketing strategy is the means by which a marketing goal is achieved, usually setting up a proposition that people will buy. There can be some confusion between the corporate strategy and the marketing strategy.

The corporate strategy focuses on the mission statement and outlines the company's purpose, objectives, resource allocation and activities. However, marketing is the most important function in determining corporate strategy and this is the reason why a separate 'marketing strategy' must be ruthlessly stuck to in all decisions taken by the firm, to give them a sustainable competitive edge.

## Managing the marketing strategy

The marketing strategy should be supported in the entire marketing process (as we saw in the previous chapter) with planning a marketing campaign. It covers marketing in its entirety. The three key supports to developing the marketing strategy at a macro level are illustrated in Figure 5.

Managing the strategy at a detailed or micro level is a continuous process, as illustrated in Figure 6.

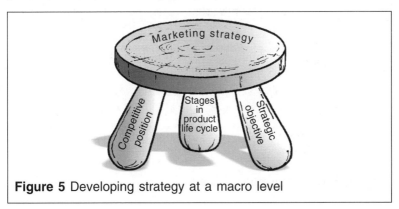

**Figure 5** Developing strategy at a macro level

## Market coverage strategies

An *undifferentiated marketing strategy* is mostly used in mass marketing, treating the entire market as one segment. This involves the same marketing mix being directed to cover the entire market. However, as incomes have increased and competition intensified the need to target market segments has risen. This involves a *differentiated marketing strategy*, by which the market is split into segments to target sales by catering for groups of consumers. For example, a leisure centre might use different strategies to target families with children and the elderly using separate marketing mixes. Differentiated marketing offers a degree of product variability, and differentiation intensifies as the product matures and the increase in sales slows down. A *concentrated marketing strategy* is seen as the final stage in the development of marketing coverage strategies, in which the marketing mix is targeted on a narrow segment of customers known as a niche, for example the holiday company 'Club 18–30'.

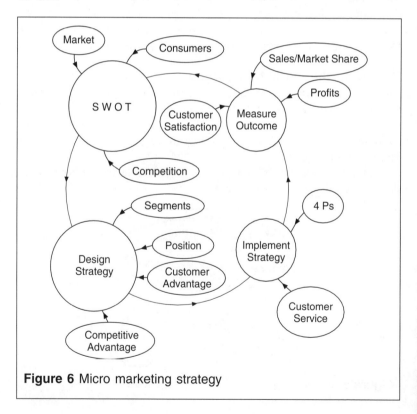

**Figure 6** Micro marketing strategy

## Positioning strategies

Customer perception is reality, and it is therefore important for any firm to understand how the market perceives their product and rivals. By reviewing their brand **positions** in relation to their rivals (as illustrated for Unilever in the Brand Positioning Map, Figure 7) companies can:

- meet perceptions head on;
- compete against a competitor for the same position;
- spot gaps in the market;
- re-position away from rival;
- reposition their own products to avoid cannibalization.

*Repositioning* can be about changing to a different market segment; changing image, quality, price or even product class. In 1995 Calvin Klein shook up the fragrance market when it marketed the first unisex scent, CK One. A successful re-positioning will only work if the customers' perception of the brand message relates to the core values of the product which they receive. A mismatch, as in the case when Babycham tried to move up-market, will fail to convince the consumer. Finally brands may decide to *deposition* by seeking to be the best at arousing universal human impulses instead of owning a niche in the market. This has been the case with gourmet foods that are aspirational, or by creating new traditions like Clarks Shoes appeal to the middle aged with their re-launch campaign: 'Act Your Shoe Size Not Your Age.'

## Unique Selling Point (USP)

At the centre of the marketing strategy will be the firm's Unique Selling Point, or **USP**. The USP positions the product in the market by differentiating it, thereby making it more desirable and distinctive to a selected target market segment than its competitors. *Differentiation* occurs when firms make their product different to gain an edge over their rivals. This difference can be in performance, design, service and perceived value for money. Delivering the position means that the product, price, place and promotional designs must all be supporting the same objective, the marketing strategy.

Some firms will have a Unique Selling Point of what they are producing, which is different to other companies, giving them a competitive edge. Another form of USP is a Unique Selling Proposition that places most emphasis on the promotional message that is being conveyed. Ultimately though a proposition will have to deliver which means that the Unique Selling Point remains central. For example,

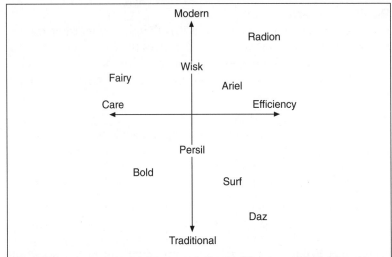

**Figure 7** Brand positioning – Unilever (Source: *Marketing Now*, Lever, Heinemann Educational, 1993)

Volvo was one of the first companies to realize that safety sells when most in the car industry were convinced customers didn't really care about a car's safety record.

It is easy for a firm to pick the wrong USP and implement it poorly with a resulting decline in sales. Firms must decide how many differences to promote and to stick to them. Trying to be the best in terms of quality, service, price, value, and the most advanced in technological developments might, by over-positioning, confuse the customer with too many position strategies. Alternatively a firm might under position if it fails to identify a strong USP.

## Strategic models

Marketing strategists will look at the overall picture of the corporation (known as its *product portfolio*) and decide whether it is to support existing brands, to remove products or to add products. This is known as Product Portfolio Analysis (sometimes known as Business Portfolio Analysis). Strategists also evaluate the strength and attractiveness of the product, market, or industry. To assist their analysis firms have used the **Boston Box**, the **GE Matrix** and the **Ansoff Matrix**.

## Benetton's USP: Humanity

MADELINE BUNTING

Marketing experts know that there are masses of products out there of much the same quality and price what they have to convince us of is not the virtues of the product, but what buying it says about you. Clever branding is about loading a product with meaning that you want to buy into. Ever since Oliviero Toscani arrived at Benetton, he has been devising shocking campaigns which illustrate one idea: our common humanity. He started simply, with a picturesque racial assortment of faces, and got bolder; he photographed a man dying of Aids surrounded by his grieving family, then it was a newborn baby covered in blood with intact umbilical cord, and even a black stallion mounting a white mare. And now, even prisoners on death row are welcomed to Benetton's human race. For all our diversity, we are human and deserve tolerance and respect, is the message. We all belong. It is a message of utopianism akin to the Puritans setting sail on the Mayflower.

Extract from 'Drowning in latte' in the *Guardian*, 24 January 2000

## The Boston Box

Developed by the Boston Consulting Group (BCG) the Boston Box (illustrated in Figure 8) provides a growth-share matrix. This allows firms to understand the position of each of their products in terms of current and projected performance. It also helps them to decide how viable the products are in terms of their strategic role and potential for growth.

The Boston Box helps the market strategist draw these conclusions by measuring the general level of growth in the product's market against their market share. If the general market growth, measured along the vertical axis, is high then it is assumed that there is enough room for all firms to expand. If it is low competition will be more intense as the firm's growth will only be achievable at the expense of rivals. Along the bottom axis the firm's market share is matched against their largest competitor in the market. If their share is low then they are in a weak position. Whereas if it is high then this means that their sales volume is greater than their rival. If it is borderline then they are joint leaders in the market. By measuring the market growth rate against their relative market share they can identify the position of their product in the market and assess what strategic decision to take.

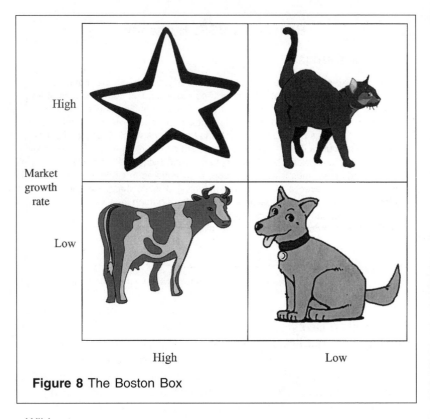

High

Market
growth
rate

Low

High                     Low

**Figure 8** The Boston Box

## Wild cat

In a market that is growing, a **wild cat** product is one that is either under-performing or is a new product that is yet to establish itself, like Digital TV (at the time of writing). The 'question mark' for this 'problem child' as these products are sometimes known, is whether to risk investing in the product to keep up with an expanding market. If a company doesn't the product might turn into a **dog**, which means they might decide to stop producing it.

## Star

If the product has a high share of a fast growing market it is known as a **star**. As a market leader product it will be well placed to grow more as the market expands, for example, organic, health and vegetarian food. Whilst stars often require finance to develop they are in a strong position as they are likely to generate cash in the future.

## Cash cow

**Cash cows** are stars that have tailed off but continue to generate large cash flows since they dominate the market in which they have matured. Examples include most established branded FMCGs (fast moving consumer goods) like Fairy, Persil or Kellogg's Cornflakes. Due to their dominant position they are able to use the cash to maintain their position by lowering costs and innovations or diverting it into less successful products.

## Dog

A dog is a product that is likely to be making a low profit, or even a loss, in a market which is unlikely to increase its share due to low market growth. The firm must decide whether investing in a dog in an intensely competitive declining market is worthwhile. Alternatively they might wait on the basis that the market might turn upwards lifting the dog into a wild cat. The firm might decide to let the dog fend for itself by withdrawing support or 'shoot the dog' by withdrawing it from the market, which was considered (apparently inadvisably) with the football game Subbuteo. A product can act as a 'guard dog' by blocking a competitor; or a 'sheep dog' by guiding customers to its more successful products, then it might also be worthwhile to persist. In this way it can be observed that each product may go through a product life cycle, which will take it through the stages from being a wild cat to a star to a cash cow to a dog.

## Product life cycle

Every product has a life cycle that takes it from before it is launched to its permanent removal. The use of **product life cycles** in marketing aids decision-making. The length and shape of the cycle will vary, from ones that last for years to those more short-lived. Most products tend to move through five phases, as illustrated in Figure 9.

1. *The product's development prior to its launch* is the first phase in which the idea of the product is born and tested until it is believed to be ready to introduce to the market. During this phase losses are often made due to high development costs. For example, the most expensive film of its time, Titanic, cost $200 million in the making.
2. *Introduction.* When the product is launched, the main priority will be to establish the product in the market place as at this stage it is what is referred to in the Boston Box as a *'wild cat'*. Sales will often be low due to distributors being unsure or unaware of the product. To overcome this advertising and/or good public relations are required during the development phase. The product will be

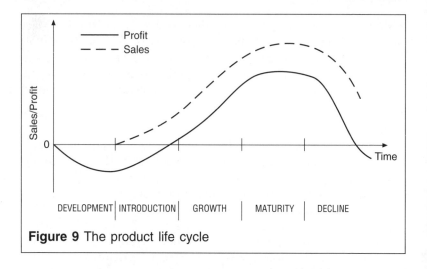

**Figure 9** The product life cycle

unlikely to make a profit due to low sales and the associated high start up costs. Current examples of products in their introductory phase include video-phones, electric cars and wall-hanging flat screen TVs.

3. *Growth*. During this phase sales will rapidly increase and the product will be seen as a '*star*' to the company. Competition will start to enter the market and could flatten the growth curve prematurely, unless defensive measures are taken. Often this competition will come from 'me-too' products, late-comers who are now wanting to jump on the bandwagon. The firm will have to decide before maturity is reached how to re-launch, modify or improve the product. Often they will have the advantage of being one step ahead of the competition, by learning from the launch what works and what doesn't. As the firm starts to experience economies of scale its profit levels will start to rise. Sunny Delight was the most successful grocery launch of the 1990s in the UK, according to *Marketing* magazine. Procter & Gamble fruit drink sales soared 5,224% in the first twelve months of its launch in 1998.

4. *Maturity*. Eventually market capacity will be reached, as there are few additional customers buying the product. The market is satiated and customers might start to tire of the product. Sales will level off and the product will be seen as a '*cash cow*' to the company, as sales are high but further growth is not expected. The organization will have to consolidate brand loyalty and successfully promote itself in the face of stiff competition. Examples include colour TVs and video players.

5. *Decline*. Eventually the same reasons why a product matures might lead to a decline in sales and profit, turning the product into a '*dog*'. The rapidity of the decline will depend on the product. If it is a passing fashion or intense competition exists then decline could be quick. A firm can decide to slow the decline by increased marketing expenditure, or to get what they can from the decline by withdrawing support expenditure and 'milking' the resulting profit from a speedy decline. Examples include typewriters, record players and black and white TVs. Selling off or deleting products that have a poor return or are costly to support might be difficult because of a firm's emotional attachment to a product with a long history, wanting to maintain a wide product range, or sunk costs in the product such as product specific machinery or training.

### Extension

To extend maturity or delay a decline in sales an extension strategy might be implemented as illustrated in Figure 10. Extension can be achieved by advertising more heavily, modifying the product by adding new features, or extending the product range. For example, Pringles introducing different flavours and packaging of their snack products. Other extension strategies are finding new uses for the product or changing its core essence. For example, Lucozade moved from being the drink that 'aids recovery' for those that are ill to being an 'energy' drink associated with sport. A further extension strategy is to encourage increased usage by introducing disposable products.

During the decline in sales a firm will have to decide whether to let the product go and remove it from the market or whether a successful *re-launch* is possible as illustrated in Figure 11. Brylcreem was

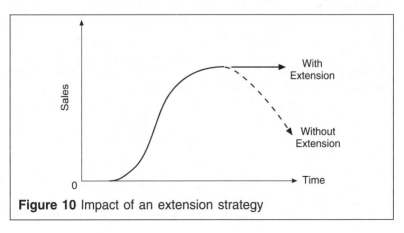

**Figure 10** Impact of an extension strategy

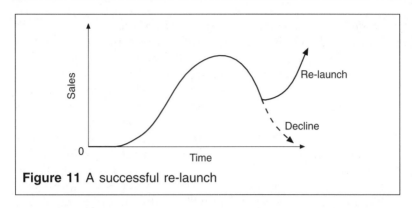

**Figure 11** A successful re-launch

successfully re-launched by the conglomerate Sara Lee, by repositioning the product and changing the marketing mix to be more youth-orientated.

The Boston box enables the marketing strategist to identify a healthy product portfolio of cows and stars and suggests how to develop a successful marketing strategy to achieve this. Once the firm has identified the product in the matrix it can then go on to decide what role it will play in the future. It can invest and increase the product's share of the market, hold the share of the market, speed up its decline by reducing support, or divest and sell it off.

The disadvantage with the Boston Box is that it does not help decide which products to invest in and assumes that cash flow is influenced primarily by market share and growth. To help the firm decide which products to invest in, the market strategist can use the GE Matrix.

## The GE Matrix

Developed by General Electric, the multinational company, the GE Matrix illustrated in Figure 12 provides a strategic business planning grid allowing firms to assess investment decisions based on the market attractiveness of their position. By looking at an 'industry attractiveness index' and a 'business strength index' the firm can make a strategic investment decision. If the firm is in zone one it will exist in a highly attractive industry and be in a strong position to increase investment. If the firm exists in zone three it is existing in an industry which is the least attractive and will have to decide whether to milk the business or divest. In zone two the firm will exist in an industry with medium attractiveness, and will have to decide whether to maintain or make selective investments.

The 'industry attractiveness index' is based on market size, profit

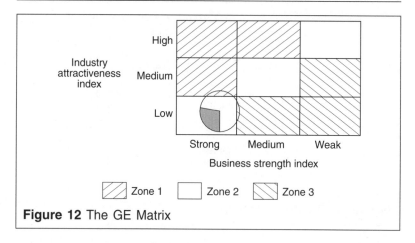

**Figure 12** The GE Matrix

margin, competition, demand, cost structure, rate of growth, legal changes, and technological change. Whereas the 'business strength index' is based on factors that determine stronger relative market share, for example, price, quality, competition, productivity, brand loyalty, sales, geographical advantage, and distribution. The Circle size represents the size of the market with the shaded area representing the market share of the firm.

The GE model, as with the Boston and other strategic models, whilst helping to analyse the current position in the market does not help the business finalize what marketing strategy to adopt. Both Boston and GE models, developed in the 1970s, can be difficult and time consuming to produce and costly to implement. They also have disadvantages in focusing more on what is currently happening than on the future. As a result poor decision-making has been associated with these portfolio-planning methods from entering a market without expertise to milking what could have been a healthy business. As a result many companies have dropped this method and switched to a more customized approach.

## The Ansoff Matrix

To overcome the problems in the Boston Box and GE Matrix with identifying growth opportunities most organizations now use the Ansoff matrix. The Matrix proposed by Ansoff in 1957 is a product-market expansion grid, which helps firms to decide which marketing strategy to adopt to maximize sales volume. It uses the age of the product and the market to produce four distinct marketing strategies (illustrated in the cells in Figure 13).

• Market penetration will be used to increase sales in the existing

| | | Product: Existing | Product: Potential |
|---|---|---|---|
| Market | Existing | Market penetration | Product development |
| | Potential | Market development | Diversification |

**Figure 13** The Ansoff Matrix

market, usually by more aggressive marketing, as persuading to buy is the first step towards creating brand loyalty. An aggressive campaign could include cutting prices or heavy promotional activity, as in the case of Häagen Dazs ice cream offering the extreme 'consumption' experience.

- Market development increases sales of an existing product by entering new markets. Brylcreem, originally used mainly by elderly men and regarded as a cash cow by SmithKline Beecham, was re-launched targeting young men when Sara Lee bought the brand in 1993. Changing the market's perception of the product image in advertising is vital to market development.
- Product development involves improving or re-launching the product into existing markets or re-packaging. Alton Towers introduced 'Oblivion' when its current range of rides was failing to attract young thrill seekers. Successful product development requires researching and implementing customer requirements to market orientate the product rather than changing the market.
- **Diversification** concerns entering a new market with a new product. This might not be a growth-orientated strategy as it helps the company to spread its risks and exploit new opportunities by changing sales or customer mix. Successful diversification is about using the firm's strengths in new areas. To do this they need to move across markets using the recognized brand name on packaging and in advertising. Richard Branson relies heavily on the 'Virgin' name to help launch new products. An alternative method of diversification is 'piggybacking' by adding a product sample to a leading brand.

Firms might also grow by expanding along their chain of distribution, which links the manufacturer to the consumer or end-user. If they acquire the capacity to produce or control their suppliers this is known as backward integration (or merger). Alternatively if they do the same with distributors, wholesalers or retailers this is known as forward integration (or merger). The objective of expanding along the chain of distribution would be the potential gain in increased quality and efficiency. Horizontal integration (or merger) is when complementary or competitive producers are bought resulting in cost savings in distribution and merchandising.

## Strategic marketing positions

The position of a firm in the market place will influence its market strategy.

Holding the position of **market leader** will require defending and expanding the total market share using the market mix, for example Coca-Cola expanding their range of products. Market leadership might rely on *cost leadership*; this is the ability to lead in changing prices as a result of greater cost minimization, productivity and sales maximization than rivals. By leading with the lowest price firms are at risk if people stop feeling that they are getting value for money. A famous example of this is when Gerald Ratner described the goods his firm sold as 'crap'. As a result, Ratner himself parted from his firm, and the firm abandoned his name. If the firm is the market leader, cost leadership can involve increasing prices as in the case of the major banks raising the cost of borrowing, the rate of interest.

A **market follower** copies the leader to survive and may innovate to challenge the leader. The main features of followers are keeping their costs low and developing a distinctive position. The main methods are cloning, imitating or adapting. Japanese firms have been very successful since the 1950s in taking apart and analysing western technological products to produce cheaper or more advanced versions.

A **market challenger** will attack the leader or weaker competitors. The objectives of a challenger will be similar to its competitors in seeking to increase market share and adopting competitive postures.

Positioning as a **market nicher** will require specializing by focusing dominating a narrow segment of the market. The aim is to maximize profit margins instead of sales volume

## Competitive postures

Often the basis for attack, defence or avoidance is by estimating how competitors are likely to react.

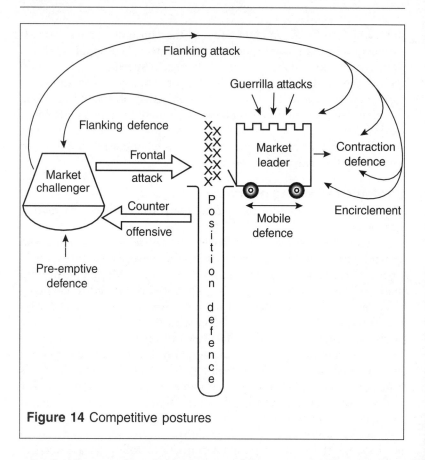

**Figure 14** Competitive postures

In deciding on the market strategy there are postures a firm can take in attacking or defending market positions as illustrated in Figure 14.

A *frontal attack* is one which attacks the market leader, using the marketing mix, on all fronts. This is a high-risk strategy that can lead to a price war. A challenger is therefore more likely to use a *guerrilla attack* making small gains by periodic attacks to harass and demoralise competitors for example using selective price cuts. *Encirclement* is another form of attack from all directions, and will make use of flanking methods.

*Out-flanking or bypassing* avoids direct engagement by leap-frogging with new technological advances; or attacking weak segments like new geographical markets; or diversifying into unrelated products in the same market to develop brand recognition.

*Defensive* postures might seem the safest but sitting tight and defending a *fixed position* risks a new product defeating the held position in the future. This is why different defensive strategies will be used:

- *Position defence* – a leader fortifies by improving or adapting their product, thus strengthening the core business especially in times of sustained attack;
- *Flanking defence* – watching weaker flanks and strengthening weak spots vulnerable to a flanking attack;
- *Pre-emptive defence* – 'the best form of defence is to attack first';
- *Counter-offensive defence* – hit back by engaging in a price war or attacking the soft underbelly of the rival going for the 'cash cow' through the weak spots;
- *Mobile defence* – by being on the move attack is avoided. Entering new markets, broadening the product range, or market diversification, can do this. By diversifying into unrelated areas strategic depth can be achieved since if one area moves into decline another might start to grow.
- *Contraction defence* -in the late eighties boom many firms ended up spreading themselves too thin, a contraction defence will therefore involve strategic withdrawal from weaker areas to the core business.

Disruptive competition can shake up a market by engaging in a costly price war and supplying to the point of over-capacity and increasing debts. An example of this is, Amazon.com books who, in their attempt to dominate the book market, are willing to make a short term loss, like other virtual companies. Most firms will therefore engage in 'well-behaved' competition playing by the rules, for example using technological advances to increase market share. It is not unusual also for firms to find it to their advantage to work co-operatively, passing on trade to firms in the same market. This does not mean collusion in the sense of firms colluding to the disadvantage of the consumer, which is illegal in the UK and Europe. If firms are 'similar general' in existing in the same geographical market it might not make sense to beat their competition out of business if this stops people coming to the area as in the case of a tourist attraction, for example.

---

```
                          KEY WORDS
Positioning                    Cash cow
USP                            Product life cycle
Boston Box                     Diversification
GE Matrix                      Market leader
Ansoff Matrix                  Market follower
Wild cat                       Market challenger
Dog                            Market nicher
Star                           Competitive postures
```

## Further reading

Danks, S. *et al.*, Chapter 8 in *Business Studies*, Letts, 1999.

Grant, J., Part 4 in *The New Marketing Manifesto*, Orion, 1999.

Kotler, P., Part One and Two in *Kotler on Marketing*, Simon & Schuster, 1999.

Zyman, S., Chapter 2 in *The End of Marketing As We Know It*, Harper Collins, 1999.

## Useful websites

Larry Chase's Web Digest For Marketers: http://wdfm.com

'Single best source for facts on the Net': www.Refdesk.com

## Essay topics

1. (a) Marketing Growth strategies have been summarized by Igor Ansoff. Identify them and describe their likely applications. [15 marks]
   (b) What are the disadvantages with using the Ansoff matrix. [10 marks]

2. (a) How does the Boston Box help a business? [10 marks]
   (b) For a given brand describe how the Boston box can be applied through the brand's life stages. [15 marks]

## Data response question

Read the article below (by Louise Proddow, marketing director, Sun Microsystems) which appeared in the *Guardian* on 11 December 1999 and then answer the questions that follow.

## It's dot com or die in the digital world

With the millennium just weeks away the key issue facing businesses large and small is how well their marketing strategies are in tune with the digital economy. Marketing in the new millennium has to be 'dot commed' by seizing the opportunities that the Internet offers. If 'dot com' is not embedded in the marketing strategy then your company has not realized the world has changed.

A couple of years ago marketers were proud when they created a website that allowed people to browse in an online brochure. Today the Internet has to be embedded 'through the line', from branding to fulfilment, from online transactions to liaising with agencies....

With product launches, think and act in Internet time. Gone are the days of annual product launches; a year in normal time is equal to three months in Internet time. Whatever your normal time to market – halve it and halve it again. Out there on the world-wide web a new start-up can hit you in a matter of weeks and, backed by venture capital funds, out-market you too. So focus on building market share and delivering added value rather than return on investment.

1. 'If *dot com* is not embedded in the marketing strategy then your company has not realized the world has changed.' Explain this statement. [5 marks]
2. Explain the USP for a Web site of your choice. [7 marks]
3. Using Boston Box analysis discuss the impact of the world-wide web on Product Life Cycles. [7 marks]
4. How can the Web result in disruptive competition and what marketing postures might companies adopt to resist this competition? [7 marks]

## Chapter Four

# Market research

*'Like a scientist designing an experiment, you have to ask the right questions.'*
Sergio Zyman (see Chapter Three, page 28)

## Market research defined

In 1960 the American Marketing Association (AMA) defined market research as:

'The systematic gathering, recording, and analysis of data about problems relating to the marketing of goods and services.'

This involves the following elements:

- Systematic – using people, equipment and procedures in an orderly way to identify and resolve a problem
- Gathering – identifying relevant information and using the appropriate method to gather data, for example, primary or secondary, observation or interviews.
- Recording and sorting – keeping clear and organized records.
- Analyzing and evaluating – making sense of the information identifying relevant trends and drawing conclusions
- Presentation – presenting timely and accurate information required by marketing decision makers to understand customers and the market.

Market research links the consumer and public to the marketer by spending time understanding competitor's and consumers' habits and motivations. Companies need this information to keep abreast of all the changes taking place in the market to be able to plan their activities and reduce uncertainty. The most common mistake for many people in business is to fail to listen to their customers on a regular basis. It is for this reason that market research is central to a market audit. The top five sectors in terms of expenditure on market research in the UK are food and drink, the media, public services and utilities, financial services and pharmaceutical companies.

## The research plan

Market research requires a market research plan as shown in Figure 15, sometimes referred to as a *Market Information Systems (MIS)*.

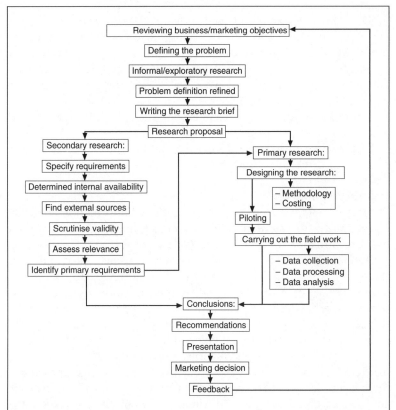

**Figure 15** Market Research Plan (Source: *Successful Market Research in a Week*, Matthew Housden, Hodder and Stoughton, 1992)

This specifies the information required and addresses how the information is to be collected, managed, analysed and presented, and finally whether further research is required.

## The research proposal

Where market research can go wrong is often because the wrong problem was identified. This can be a result of insufficient attention being paid to the current objectives of the business. It is for this reason that a market research company or department will put together a research brief to confirm what the research will seek to find. This may involve 'exploratory research' using preliminary data to clarify or identify a problem.

Descriptive research will then provide a deeper understanding of an issue and with a specific brief a large-scale survey can be undertaken. Market research can be made easier by splitting the research up into market trends, price changes, promotional activity, product and packaging development, place, sales, and the external environment. The more in depth a company wants its market research to be the more likely it is to use outside bodies such as research agencies and consultants.

The research proposal will consider the best mix of secondary or primary research to be undertaken.

## Primary research

**Primary** or field **research** is first hand gathered information about the market and is therefore more likely to meet directly the needs of the business. Primary research can be undertaken by:

*Observation* – This involves observing customer behaviour from the number of customer responses to those attracted to a new promotion. Research instruments and equipment can be used to observe consumer behaviour and gather observational data including: CCTV (Closed Circuit Television used primarily for store security), tally counters, or EPOS (Electronic Point of Sale) equipment that uses bar codes to observe sale trends. A form of observational research is 'test marketing' which is causal or predictive, meaning that they test if there is a cause and effect relationship between actions and their outcome to be able to make predictions. For example, the response of sales to a new promotional campaign.

*Consumer panels* involve a group of consumers who record their purchases and/or media habits in a diary. A C Nielsen, for example, undertakes *continuous research* in the UK, in tracking retail purchases by consumers.

*Focus Groups* use a small number of carefully selected people who are interviewed in depth to obtain high quality detailed responses about the target market.

*Questionnaires and Surveys* – can take different forms to elicit the most suitable information. Personal one to one interviews can take place by doing door-to door visits; or stopping people on the street or inside a shop. Customers can also be contacted using CATI (Computer Assisted Telephone Interviewing) which enables the telephone interviewer to have customer information at hand and the ability to enter information gathered directly. Feedback forms are another type of survey using promotional mailings, products sold or the Internet. **Questionnaires** can be structured to provide descriptive

---

### Political focus groups

The Labour Party in the General Election of 97 made heavy use of focus groups of 1992 Conservative voters who were considering switching to Labour. According to Philip Gould, who conducted most of these focus groups: 'I like to use the groups to develop and test ideas.'

*Source:* P Gould, 'The Unfinished Revolution', 1999, Little, Brown and Company

information or unstructured to be able to probe deeply. Questions can either be:

*Open-ended* using a variety of methods such as:

- completely unstructured – respondent can reply in any way
- word association – first word that comes to mind
- sentence completion – often used in competitions
- story completion – longer introduction provided
- picture completion – respondents fill in an empty voice bubble of someone speaking in a set environment
- thematic apperception tests – these are theme based tests where respondents are shown a picture and asked to make up a story, with a theme based on their perception of what they see.

or

*Closed-ended* using the following methods:

- Dichotomous – meaning two answers are offered for example Yes or No
- Multiple choice – three or more answers are offered as options to choose from
- **Likert scale** – used to indicate customers agreement or disagreement with a statement, for example:

This product is the best in the market:

| Strongly Disagree | Disagree | No opinion | Agree | Strongly Agree | |
|---|---|---|---|---|---|
| ❑ | ❑ | ❑ | ❑ | ❑ | (Please tick) |

- Semantic scale – means that respondents select feelings between two bipolar words (expressing opposite views), for example:

How do you feel about our service?

| Strongly Like | Like | Don't mind | Dislike | Strongly dislike | |
|---|---|---|---|---|---|
| ❑ | ❑ | ❑ | ❑ | ❑ | (please tick) |

- Importance scale – level of importance is indicated
- Rating scale – usually indicated from poor to excellent
- Intention to buy scale – from definitely not to most certainly.

Closed-ended questions have the advantage of having a higher response rate and being able translate into coded data, which it is easier to observe trends with. Since questionnaires are time consuming it is important to *pilot test* the questionnaire before undertaking the full survey to spot errors or improvements to be made. Pilots can also help identify 'filter questions' to encourage people to be more forthcoming.

The largest survey in Britain is the National **Census** in which information is gathered on every household every ten years. The National Census is usually used as a source of secondary information. For firms, they might undertake a census that involves questioning everybody in a particular market.

Omnibus surveys are surveys on behalf of a number of companies. This allows clients to share the costs of research by pooling questions. All questions are put on a single questionnaire. Each individual client's results are processed in such a way as to ensure that each party only sees their own data. BMRB's weekly access survey is a weekly omnibus survey for a wide range of companies.

## Sampling

With primary research surveys *sampling* is necessary to obtain information on the target market and ensure statistically reliable information so as not to skew market research results. This means that researchers need to choose a sample frame that includes: who to sample; the size of the sample; and whether to choose the sample using a probability or non-probability method.

**Probability sampling** includes:

*Random sampling* – by choosing people or customers at random, every member of the population has an equal chance of selection. For example, picking people at random from a telephone directory.

*Stratified Random Sampling* – divides the population into mutually exclusive groups or segments from which people are randomly chosen. A larger sample can be allocated to a group, which matter more, for example in an election swing voters.

*Cluster sampling* – occurs when the market is divided into areas which are then randomly selected. In the selected area respondents are randomly selected. This saves time and expense by avoiding covering too large an area.

Probability sampling can be costly and time-consuming hence '**non-probability sampling**' is used as an alternative. This includes:

*Quota sampling* – this requires the interviewer to find and interview a number of people from each market segment, for example age groups. The problem is that those chosen might not accurately represent most people in that segment.

*Judgement sampling* – requires the researcher to use their judgement to accurately select respondents required, for example identifying teenagers on a high street.

*Convenience sampling* – involves interviewing anyone available no matter what his or her background, as a result this is the easiest method.

## Processing the data

Without **statistical analysis** data can mean anything. Statistical analysis can summarize and provide a useful, understandable and concise account of the key characteristics emerging from the data. By noting trends between different sets of data it can be observed if a significant relationship or difference exists. The ability to make statements and predictions, based on the statistics about the target market or population, is known as inferential statistics.

To make large amounts of information concise and descriptive a central tendency is required, which is the *average* of a set of data. This can be achieved using a number of different methods:

- The mode occurs the most frequently for example 2, 4, 4, 5, 8, 9 = 4.
- The median is the middle value of data when placed in numerical order for example 2, 4, 4, 5, 8, 9 = 5. If there are two numbers in the middle you work out the mean of those two numbers.
- The mean is the sum of data added up divided by the amount of data gathered for example 2+4+4+5+8+9 = 42/6 = 7.

The dispersion or spread of the data around these averages helps to describe the data. The average however may be misleading if the average does not reflect a set of data whose values are very widely spread. To indicate the full range of data to get the wider picture the following measures of dispersion are useful:

a) The range – measures the difference between the largest and smallest values in the set of data. However, it can be misleading if the smallest value is rare whilst the larger values are more common.

b) **Quartiles** are useful in overcoming misleading information given the spread of data in a range. The range is divided into four parts (quartiles) each containing the same number of variables, by finding the median and using it to classify values as above or below the median. The range of data can be divided into different parts, for example quintiles will split the range into five parts. In the case of quartiles, the upper and lower quartiles are then further subdivided on the basis of the median for each class. The difference between the upper quartile and lower is known as the inter-quartile range.

Quartiles can still be misleading by over-generalising and failing to consider every single data value. By looking at the deviation of each value from the mean this problem can be overcome.

c) Mean deviation is a simple and easy to understand method of dispersion analysis. After finding the mean (central tendency) for the set of data, deviation from the mean is then calculated by subtracting the data from the mean. These absolute deviations are then added up (ignoring negative signs) providing the mean deviation for the set of data.

Mean deviation =
$$\frac{\text{absolute difference between each value of x and the mean}}{\text{number of values in the set}}$$

d) **Standard deviation** provides a standardized measure of the distribution of the data around the mean value. To calculate this, statisticians:

1. find the arithmetic mean of the distribution
2. find the deviation of the value of all items from the arithmetic mean
3. square each deviation
4. add the squared deviations
5. divide the total of the squared deviations by the number of items. The result is the variance
6. find the square root of the variance. The result is the standard deviation.

The advantage of this method is that it is suitable for further statistical analysis. Indeed, it is the most widely used measure of dispersion, particularly in sampling theory.

## Secondary Research

Secondary information uses existing sources of information that have been gathered in the market and published. It has the general advantage of being relatively cheap and quick to gather, for example a company using its own sales figures. **Secondary research** is sometimes referred to as desk research because it concerns research gathered without going out of the organization by using internal or external sources.

### Internal
Internal information might include:
- Information on the size of your market.
- Sales records, information from re-sellers on consumer reactions and responses to your product and competitors.
- How customers prefer to pay (computer firm Dell's ambition is to get everyone paying for its computers by credit card on the Internet).
- Which type of customers are impulsive buyers, habitual buyers or passing trade?
- What is the profitability or turnover for each type of consumer?
- Customer satisfaction and service records provided by the Customer Service Department.

### External
External information is vital as it informs a company how they stand in relation to their external market environment: its competitors and political, economic, social and technological changes.
External information might include:

- Government information. In the UK this is available from the Office for National Statistics and is a good source for desk research as it identifies national trends contained in reports listed on their Web site.
- Independent Forecasting Groups. For example, the Henley Centre provides monthly reports of important trends and development in all major consumer markets in the UK.
- Company reports. These are available from Companies House who provide contact information, company reports and financial information.
- Newspapers. For example, the *Financial Times* might review a certain sector of business or a rival firm and latest developments
- Trade associations. The BMRA (British Market Research Association) provides information on market research spent across industries.
- Trade press and magazines. *Marketing Week* is the leading UK weekly magazine for marketing.
- Market research companies. Mintel is perhaps the best known analyst of consumer information, producing market intelligence

reports into consumer purchasing and usage habits.
- European research. Euromonitor is a major provider of market analysis on products and services in major industrial economies including Germany, France and the UK.

Most external information is available direct from the firm, organization or publisher (including CD-ROM formats); libraries; and online via the Internet.

## Problems with market research

The value of the information gathered and presented is found in its use. To be useful it needs to be concise and provide the right information at the right time. However market intelligence gathering can fail when:

- developments in the market environment cause research gathered to be quickly out of date;
- personnel fail to pass information on or gather accurate information;
- information gathered on competitors is irrelevant.

### The disadvantages with secondary research are that:
- the information provided might already be out of date
- it might not provide the information that you want
- it is most likely to be available to competitors
- the information might be unobtainable, as under the **Data Protection Act** information about people registered on a database must not be passed on to a second party without their express permission.

### Disadvantages of primary research
In primary research there is often a conflict between **quantitative** versus **qualitative** research. By undertaking quantitative research the aim is to cover as many people in the market as possible. This has the advantage of being quick and cheap but the disadvantage of lacking detailed information. With qualitative more in-depth research via discussion groups or individual interviews is required to understand people's motivation, feelings and behaviour. The advantage with qualitative research is that it is exploratory and interactive, thereby allowing more in depth research of potential consumer perceptions. The disadvantage with qualitative research is that it is time consuming and can be expensive.

As a general rule the more accurate the method of primary research the more expensive and time consuming it can become. Primary research that takes a long time to collect and analyze can also become rapidly out of date. Results are also restricted to the questions asked, the accurate recording of responses and the sample used. Additionally the external environment and other factors will influence the accu-

## Quantitative versus qualitative

RUPERT HOWELL

Too often we are swayed by phrases such as 'research proves' without studying the quality of that research.

I am a passionate believer in good research, but I am deeply frustrated by the quality of advertising research available today, particularly quantitative research.

Most models of quantitative research for advertising are based on judging a certain type of ad – logical propositions, side-by-side demonstrations, very simple messages – but are completely inadequate when we're talking about complex emotional messages, particularly in a multi-media environment. Where's the new product development in the market research industry?

I know some great advertising ideas that have died simply because, in the rigorous atmosphere of pre-testing, people's instant response is often one of rejection. This is a quite understandable defence mechanism. After all, we are nearly always trying to change people's behaviour and they resist that. Too many quantitative researchers still tend to see advertising as some sort of mechanical treatment of people's machine-like minds. In my view, response to communication messages isn't instantaneous. It happens over time.

To change people's opinions we often have to polarize response to create dialogue, giving the brand and its message greater stature. This means that the communication doesn't necessarily have to be liked to have an effect.

Researchers have got to be prepared to dismiss 'likeability' as the key measure. Good ads are about strength of impact. They've got to challenge the comfortable behaviour the consumer currently enjoys. Few researchers are genuinely willing to go down this road.

I'm more interested in which ad people are still talking about at the end of the research discussion rather than which ad they say they like the most. Anita Roddick once described market research as like looking in the rear-view mirror: 'It tells me where I've been, but not where I'm going.' But good qualitative research should be like putting the headlights on – showing you where you can go. But there's too little good qualitative research at the moment. Most of it just seems to reflect the status quo.

Researchers sometimes exaggerate their findings to maximize their importance. Alternatively, some researchers prefer gathering information rather than interpreting it. Not enough research takes place in 'real time'. Surely it's better to conduct research in the decision-making environment – the pub, the supermarket, the garage forecourt – rather than around a coffee table heaving with crisps and warm white wine.

Extract from 'Researched to death' in the *Guardian*, 10 April 2000

racy of the results from the use of the script to the honesty and willingness of respondents especially when it comes to personal details. If the length of the survey is too long inaccuracies might slip in as interviewees tire. Research is not an exact science so the ability to interpret and use the results, and the follow up of how research has been used are very important. In the end the acid test of primary research is whether it has helped the client, by for example increasing sales.

## Legal restrictions on market research

The Data Protection Act (1984) and the new EU Data Protection legislation govern personal information gathered from interviewees during the course of research. The use of secondary research information is protected under the Copyright, Designs and Patents Act (1988); and many general laws are also applicable for example the Trade Descriptions Act (1968). The Market Research Society in the UK operates a Code of Conduct, which protects confidentiality, identifying interviewers and holding information. The Marketing Standards Board is also responsible for setting appropriate standards to be upheld.

---

### KEY WORDS

| | |
|---|---|
| Market information systems | Non-probability sampling |
| Primary research | Statistical analysis |
| Focus groups | Quartiles |
| Questionnaires | Standard deviation |
| Likert scale | Secondary research |
| Census | Data Protection Act |
| Sampling | Quantitative research |
| Probability sampling | Qualitative research |

---

## Further reading

Housden, M., *Successful Market Research in a week*, BIM, 1992.

Kinnear, T and Taylor, J.R., *Marketing research: an applied approach*, McGraw Hill, 1996.

Marcousé, I., Chapter 4, 5 and 7 in *Business Calculations and Statistics*, Longman, 1994.

Marcousé, I., Unit 4 in *Business Studies*, Hodder & Stoughton, 1999.

## Useful websites

UK Government secondary sources: www.statistics.gov.uk
European research: www.euromonitor.com

## Essay topics

1. (a) How can field research be gathered? [10 marks]
   (b) Discuss the advantages and disadvantages of each method. [15 marks]
2. Identify the main sources of desk research. Explain the benefits and limitations of using desk research in making marketing decisions. [15 marks]

## Data response question

This task is based on a question set by AEB in 1999. Study the data below and then answer the questions that follow overleaf.

### The art of the new soft sell

There is an information revolution taking place in Britain which will allow advertisers and retailers to know *not only what we buy and where we buy it*, but also where we live and details of our *credit rating*. A combination of computerised mapping software, *census data* and *loyalty cards* is giving the marketing industry an unprecedented opportunity to gain information on the characteristics of customers purchasing a wide range of products.

Observers have commented that supermarket loyalty cards are about much more than giving loyalty points. They are a major and on-going form of *primary market research* giving rise to huge amounts of data on consumers and their preferences. Data accumulated in this way can allow firms to *analyse market segments and enable extrapolation of trends and sales forecasts*. The information technology revolution has assisted firms which engage in *scientific marketing*.

The advertising agency, *International Post Management*, which represents companies such as *Imperial Tobaco and Tesco*, is offering clients maps of postal-code areas to show occupants' preferences from vodka to airline destinations to life assurance policies.

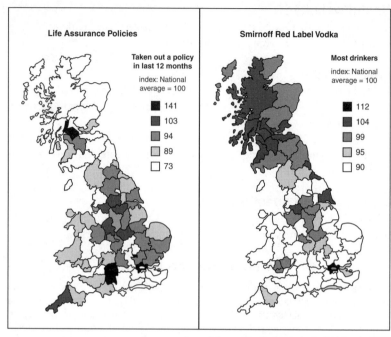

Source: adapted from *The Independent*, 17 March 1997

Market potential of life assurance policies and Smirnoff Red Label Vodka in the UK


1. What is meant by:
   (a) 'primary market research' [2 marks]
   (b) 'scientific marketing' [2 marks]
2. Explain why companies might choose to forecast their sales. [5 marks].
3. A number of supermarkets have introduced loyalty card schemes whereby customers receive awards according to the level of their expenditure with the company. Examine the factors a supermarket might consider before introducing such a scheme. [7 marks]
4. Many companies now have access to detailed data on their customers. Discuss the possible implications of this for a company when taking marketing decisions. [9 marks]

## Chapter Five

# Product

*'The best ad is a good product'*
Alan H. Meyer, quoted in Robert I. Fitzhenry, *The Fitzhenry &*
*Whiteside Book of Quotations*, Cardada, 1993

## Product definition

A product is a pure **good** or a **service**, or a mixture of both, which offers *tangible* or *intangible* benefits that individuals or organizations are willing to pay for or reward in another way to acquire, view, use or consume to meet their wants or needs.

*Tangible benefits* are physical in communicating the benefits of the product, for example design, packaging, features and branding are more visible in goods. *Intangible benefits* are those not gained physically such as customer care or service delivery.

Goods also tend to be *durable* as they can be used several times, for example cars and electrical products will usually last for a number of years. Most services, like leisure and tourism, are *non-durable* or perishable in that they cannot be stored for future use; for example a spare seat on an aeroplane cannot be transferred to the next flight. Services are inseparable as the service is being produced at the same time it is consumed. For example, in teaching a class the education service being produced by the teacher is being consumed by the students at the same time. Finally, services tend to be heterogeneous. As all people are different they are likely to require and experience different services, although the same level of standards might be maintained.

Most products have features of a good and a service. In 1999, for example, concern about the high price of cars sold in Britain was justified by the car industry by the high level of customer service and after sales support.

## Product levels

It is important therefore to distinguish between the **core product,** **actual product** and the **augmented product,** as illustrated in Figure 16. The core product is the core benefit or services the product provides. The actual product is the quality, features, styling, brand name and packaging of the product. The augmented product is the 'add

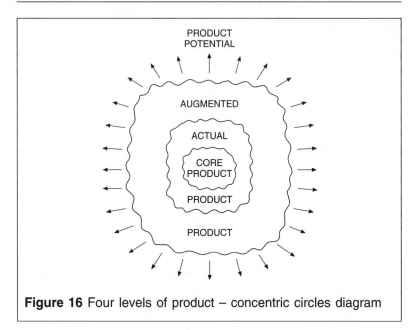

**Figure 16** Four levels of product – concentric circles diagram

on' extras to increase the satisfaction and benefits the buyer receives for example credit, after sales service, delivery, warrantees, guarantees, or insurance. Added to this is the *product potential* of what it could possibly do in the future, for instance with computers their capacity to take on new software is the product's potential.

## Consumer products

Consumer products can come in the following forms:

- *Convenience products* which are frequently purchased inexpensive items that require little choice, for example a loaf of bread.
- *Shopping products* that people take more time and effort in selecting and purchasing as with clothes.
- Speciality products that are unique and require considerable effort from the consumer to obtain, for example a music CD or designer eye glasses.
- *Unsought products* which consumers are unaware of or don't often think about as in the case of emergency products like a plumber.

## Product mix

It is rare for a manufacturer or retailer to have one product; instead they are more likely to have a portfolio or **mix of products**. The portfolio will need to appeal to different market segments, as in the case

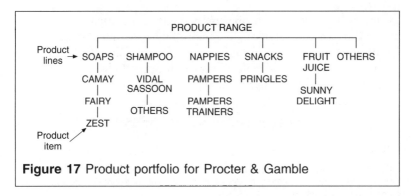

**Figure 17** Product portfolio for Procter & Gamble

of car manufacturers or insurance companies.

A product portfolio, as illustrated in Figure 17, will include the product range of all product lines offered by a firm. *Product lines* group up products closely related to each other based on technology, customers or the market. A product range can be extended, for example a new line of perfumes for men being offered by a perfume company. Along production lines each individual product or brand is known as the *product item*.

## Product line decisions

The length of product lines will depend on the objectives of the firm. They may want to offer a 'full-line' offering a variety of items or to be an up-market provider aiming only at the expensive end of the product line. In both cases most product lines tend to lengthen over time. The main reason for this lengthening is that adding items can increase product line profitability. However if the product line is too long removing items might increase profitability.

Product lines can be lengthened either by stretching or filling:

### Stretching

Stretching involves extending lines beyond their current market either upwards by charging for higher quality; or downwards by selling at bargain basement prices to a mass market. An advantage with product line **extensions** downward is that the product items can act as 'traffic builders.' By promoting models at the lower end the firm can attract consumers who then trade upwards. In the case of a car maker wanting to build brand loyalty they can encourage consumers to trade up to more expensive models as they get older, earn more and raise a family. However an organization needs to be careful when expanding its product range downward of *product cannibalization* when the sale of a new product affects the sale of an existing product. For example, by offering a cheaper mobile phone a company might risk slowing down the sales of their more expensive models instead of eating into the sales of cheaper rivals. Often a firm will extend in both directions, for example Sony has produced cheaper and more upmarket versions of their personal tape player, the Walkman.

## Unilever culls product portfolio

JULIA FINCH

Unilever is to axe 1,200, or 75% of its 1,600 consumer brands and throw its multimillion-pound marketing muscle behind just 400 high-growth products, the company has announced.

Unilever – whose products range from soap and food to Calvin Klein fragrances – intends to focus on creating powerful global brand names. All brands that are not among the two top sellers in their market segment will be ditched, and within the remaining 400 a smaller number of 'power brands' expected to grow at 6–8% a year will be selected for extra support.

The 1,200 names to be axed in the next five years will be divided into two groups. A spokesman said: 'There are those that will be sold and those that we will hang on to and milk. The cash they generate will then be put behind the big brands. Eventually they will just wither on the vine.'

Neither the power brands nor the names to be axed have been revealed but the shake-up is likely to lead to the disappearance of many well-known products. Among those that could eventually vanish are Bigga peas, Red Mountain instant coffee, Crisp 'n' Dry cooking oil, Sunlight washing-up liquid, Lux and Pears soaps, and SR toothpaste. Few are expected to be sold.

The company's Sure and Lynx deodorants could also soon be history. They are British brands and are known as Rexona and Axe in other markets. Unilever is likely to try to change names such as these, following the example set by confectionery manufacturers, who have proved brand names can be successfully altered. Marathon, for example, became Snickers and Opal Fruits recently was renamed Starburst.

The new strategy to boost the company's flagging sales growth was outlined at a meeting of City analysts and investors in London yesterday by Niall Fitzgerald, Unilever's chairman.

He told the audience that only a quarter of Unilever's brands provided 90% of turnover and that disposing of the other three-quarters would lead to a more efficient supply chain and reduced costs which could save £1bn within three years. . . . .

Mr Fitzgerald held up Unilever's Dove soap as an example of 'what we are seeking to achieve on a broader scale'. In 1991 the brand was a soap sold in 13 countries. Today it is on the market in 75 countries, it has expanded into skin care and deodorant lines and Unilever claims it is the 'leading cleansing brand in the world'. Dove sales have grown from $350m to $800m.

'Dove will soon become a billion-dollar brand,' said Mr Fitzgerald. 'It is well on its way to becoming a genuinely global brand icon.'

Extract from 'Unilever washes hands of 1,200 brands', The *Guardian*, 22 September 1999

*Filling*

An alternative is filling which lengthens the product line by plugging holes in the market, as in the case of offering a mid-market product when an upmarket and down market product is currently being offered.

However, cannibalization and customer confusion can occur if filling is over-done which is when a firm offers too many versions of their product. To overcome confusion of revamp product line a company might decide to modernize it either using piecemeal methods like changing or phasing out one item, or as a whole by for example changing the entire brand image.

A healthy product portfolio offers a balance of new and established products. It is essential for a firm's survival, as too many new products could prove too risky a strategy. In the case of Unilever they applied the 80:20 principle, (that 80 percent of their profits flow from 20 percent of their products), by culling their brands.

## Product design

**Product design** is often neglected at the expense of manufactures. Yet design can be used to obtain a 'competitive differential advantage' (CDA). By using design to get ahead of the competition, a firm can use premium pricing effectively, by charging a higher price for the product. The key to product design, as an effective part of the marketing mix, is to cause disruption in the market, by shouting out in a crowded market the products benefits.

The design of a product communicates its technical design including quality, use, and reliability, to its aesthetic design with eye catching appeal visual appeal. Tetley was able to become in one year the tea brand leader taking over from PG Tips, who had dominated the market for thirty-five years. It did so by introducing round tea bags, which have no intrinsic vale.

Product design can also make use of **'value analysis;'** by the careful study of how redesigning, standardization or methods of production can cut costs and improve quality. Value analysis is also supported by *'customer value analysis.'* This uses primary research to indicate what benefits customers value and how they rate the competition.

Product design can go badly wrong if not tested properly. Unilever's 'biggest marketing setback in the company's history' (Unilever Chairman, Sir Michael Perry) occurred in 1994 when it launched Persil Power, which was found to rot some clothes. As a result the Power sub-brand was removed, but innovations elsewhere like the launch of Persil tablets in April 1998, the most successful brand launch of 1998, means that the Persil brand continued to be successful.

## Packaging

**Packaging** is sometimes referred to as the fifth P of the marketing mix, as successful marketing is about ensuring *product differentiation*. In the eyes of the consumer what makes a product different will make it stand out from the rest. In this respect it also matches another P of marketing by making a 'personal connection'.

Packaging is a key feature of any product, as the container or wrapping serves many functions:

- Protecting the item from damage, preserving freshness and ensuring health and safety.
- Targeting different segments, for example family size.
- Enhancing brand image.
- Adding value by its aesthetic appeal to consumers i.e. what it looks like.
- Labelling provides information at the point of sale, such as ingredients, nutrition, and recycling. Some labelling will be a legal requirement or best practice for example health and safety warnings, use by dating, volume, and the producers address.
- Promoting special offers and inviting customers to explore the product by using special feature, for example coupons, instant win tags, or 'cause related marketing' like Tesco's 'Computers for Schools' campaign.

Packaging must fit in to the marketing mix in terms of its cost and ease of manufacture, storage, distribution and display.

Packaging has come under increased environmental concerns in dealing with waste reduction and recycling. A recent European Directive has said that at least half of packaging must be recoverable and at least a quarter recyclable. Some countries have gone further than this, such as Denmark.

## Branding

A **brand** is any name, term, sign, style, symbol or design or combination that distinguishes one product from another in the eyes of customers. Every brand contains a unique selling point, which is underpinned by its rational and biological dimensions. Brands also contain an emotional selling proposition. This 'non-biological' dimension relates to the brand's 'personality.' In the new marketing age 'A brand is a popular idea or set of ideas that people live by' (*The New Marketing Manifesto*, p15), like Delia Smith's Cookery set or The Body Shop. In the world of fast moving consumer goods (**FMCGs** are convenience and impulse goods like chocolate), the brand is everything. Powerful brands command strong consumer loyalty for a product that is not easy to copy or be damaged by rivals. In the UK the top three brands in 1999 based on sales were:

1. Coca-Cola
2. Walkers Crisps
3. Persil                                      (Source: A C Nielsen)

To be successful a brand's name must communicate the products benefits and quality, and be easy to pronounce, recognize and remember. In the global economy brand names must increasingly be able to translate in to other languages without causing embarrassment or offence. When the Vauxhall 'Nova' was launched in Spain it caused some embarrassment for the company since 'Nova' sounds Spanish for 'doesn't work.'

## Legal protection

To maintain its distinctive competitive advantage a brand must also be capable of registration and legal protection so long as no there is no similar branding currently in existence or the brand is generic. In fact the very success of a brand might threaten the company's right to the name by becoming generic, as in the case of cellophane or shredded-wheat.

To ensure legal protection of their intellectual property rights of the brand a firm can apply to the Patent Office in the UK, to register patents, trade marks and designs.

**Patents** are concerned with protecting the technical and functional aspects of products and processes, and are usually associated with inventions. Patents are territorial rights, for example a UK Patent will only give the holder rights within the United Kingdom.

**Trade marks**™ legally identify a product's ownership over any 'sign' that can distinguish the products of one trader from those of another, and be represented graphically. A sign includes words, logos, and sometimes sounds and smells. In 1995 Coca-Cola became the first product to register a 3-D depiction in the UK, when it registered its contour bottle. A trade mark is used as a marketing tool so that customers can recognize the product of a particular trader.

**Designs** give companies monopoly rights for the outward appearance of an article or a set of articles of products.

*Copyrights* provide automatic legal rights, which do not need to be registered. These rights apply to the owners of creative work including original literary works, photographs, musical works, and films.

*International Trade Mark* registration is essential to gain protected access to foreign markets. A single application is now required to cover the whole of the European Union with a Community Trade Mark.

## Types of brand names

Brand names can be *descriptive*, for example Hoover or Yellow Pages; *associative* where there is an indirect link, for example Burger King; or *free-standing* where there is no relation to the product, as with Kodak.

Branding can be *generic* or use a *blanket family* name that covers an entire brand range as with Tesco, Bodyshop, or Heinz. *Extended* brand names cover related product lines. For example, Dettol is the antiseptic category's key brand covering liquids, foams, sprays, plasters, soaps, mouthwash, and other related products. Extended brands can also cover unrelated products. For instance, Virgin has included records, cola, trains, and personal finance amongst its branded products in the past. Alternatively a company might decide to have a range of *individual* different brands rather than one brand name covering all, for example Procter and Gamble as illustrated in Figure 18. In doing so it is undertaking *discreet* branding by ensuring that if one brand is unsuccessful it does not drag the other products down.

Another form of branding is *endorsement*. This takes place when a logo is placed on different products, as with Cadbury's range of chocolates. Lastly *manufacturer* branding occurs when companies license their brand names for royalties, as in the case of toys for Star Wars – The Phantom Menace or Pokémon.

## Advantages of branding

For consumers branding brings a number of advantages. Branding makes it easier to shop as it is easier for consumers to locate the product they are after. This does not apply though when the consumer is not interested in particular brands or in a crowded market which makes it increasingly difficult for a brand to differentiate itself.

Brand competition 'adds value' to products for consumers in terms of improved quality, product features, information, and has in some circumstances provided more choice between competing brands, for example Ariel versus Persil or PG tips against Tetleys.

For manufacturers, the main advantage is the increased sales brand loyalty can bring. Branding also helps manufacturers gain leverage over retailers who become reliant on a leading brand. For example, retailers will follow a manufacturer's instructions on placing and promoting a leading brand in their stores.

To retailers the advantages of branding are that they are more likely to sell brand names. In the case of retailers who use their own name brands, it acts as a constant reminder to the customer associating the product with the shop. For example, with supermarkets like Safeways this is known as 'retail in a tin'.

## Brand strategies

A *multiproduct **branding strategy*** will use the reputation a brand holds in one product category into other product categories, as in the case of Virgin. It is estimated that new products launched under an existing brand name cost thirty-five percent less to launch compared to launching a new brand. The danger is that if the new product fails it will damage the brand name, altering its meaning and personality, or reducing its credibility as in the case of Levi's attempt to launch a range of suits in the 1980s.

An alternative strategy is to develop more than two separate brands in the same product category, known as *intermediary or multi-branding*. In selling an alternative detergents Procter & Gamble hope to: increase total sales; increase shelf space in retail outlets; develop healthy competition; attract different market segments and capture 'brand switchers.' Brand switchers are people who change their brand loyalty. The risk is that the producer might spread their resources too thin and that the new brand will cannibalize their other brand instead of taking business away from competitors.

## New product development

**New products** are developed in a number of ways. Firms can revive old products or acquire new products by buying an established brand as in the case of Brylcreem, or merging with another company. Another way to develop new products is through imitations of established products. Japanese firms have excelled in adapting established products, as in the case of Sony. Whilst Bell Laboratories had developed the transistor for industrial use, it was Sony who in 1955 achieved their first international success by seeing the potential for transistors in portable radios.

Innovation is the most risky form of new product development but often one that offers the most potential in terms of growth. For the company '3M,' specialization in innovation has provided a path to growth, as new products are its lifeblood. The most famous case for 3M is the story of Post-It notes. These were stumbled on by accident after 'Spencer Silver' a researcher in 3M failed to produce adhesive glue. The semi adhesive substance he was to discard became useful for Post-It notes that don't tear the surface they are attached to.

New product development usually goes through a number of stages to ensure a successful launch with plenty of market research into generating and testing ideas, and refining the marketing strategy. However the cautionary tale is that ninety percent of new products fail in the development process and many new products launched will not live beyond a year.

## Alternative product life cycle

A **product life cycle**, as shown in Figure 9 in Chapter 3, is unlikely to go through such a smooth trajectory. Regular changes in the direction of sales are likely, and not always easily explained, and the timing of each stage will differ. Also different product life cycles exist for different industries like the motor industry, product classes like diesel cars, product forms like people carriers and product brands like Volvo. The main alternative product life cycles, as illustrated in Figure 18, are:

a) Short lived fads as illustrated in Figure 18a. Fashions, such as Pokémon, will see a sharp increase and decline in sales. The pace at which a product grows often indicates a fad. Fads frequently hit younger consumers since 'When kids get involved with something they like to live it,' according to Nintendo's marketing director for the UK commenting on the Pokémon phenomenon (Shannon O'Neil, Nintendo USA Marketing Chief, *Observer* Magazine 26 Sept 99 p19).

b) Innovative products, Figure 18b, will have a long introduction period as it will take customers time to be aware and accept the product, as in the case of some new medicines.

c) Trend or style products like the one illustrated in Figure 18c are those which are successfully re-launched or come and go, examples being flares, Lucozade, Star Wars – the movies, and Ovaltine.

d) Imitative 'me-too' products, like those that imitated Walkmans personal stereo players, tend to enter the growth period quickly as illustrated in Figure 18d.

e) Product failures, like Sinclair's C5, do not enter the growth phase as shown in Figure 18e.

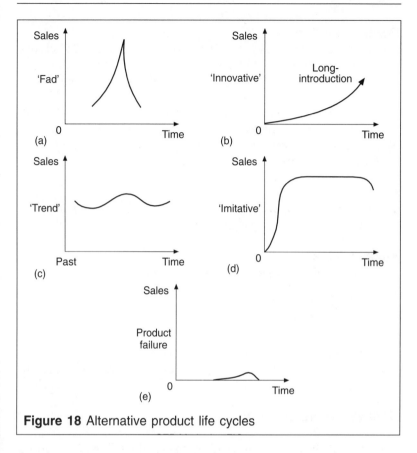

**Figure 18** Alternative product life cycles

The shape and stage of the product will influence its marketing strategy, for example what price changes to make.

| KEY WORDS | |
|---|---|
| Goods/services | FMCGs |
| Core, actual, augmented product | Patents |
| Product mix | Trade marks ™ |
| Brand extensions | Designs |
| Product design | Copyrights |
| Value analysis | Brand strategies |
| Packaging | New product development |
| Branding | Product life cycles |

## Further reading

Clifton, R. and Maughan, E., *The Future of Brands* – 25 Visions, Macmillan Business, 2000.

Fletcher, W., Chapter 11 in *Advertising Advertising*, Profile Books, 1999.

Grant, J., *The New Marketing Manifesto – The 12 Rules for Building Successful Brands in the 21st Century*, Orion, 1999.

Marcousé, I. and Lines, D., Unit 6 Even Levi's can make mistakes in *Business Case Studies*, Longman, 1999.

## Useful websites

The Design Council: www.design-council.org.uk

The Patent Office: www.patent.gov.uk/

## Essay topics

What are the advantages of brand names to:

1. (a) consumers [8 marks]
   (b) retailers [8 marks]
   (c) the manufacturers [7 marks]
2. (a) Why would a company like Unilever have several brands in the same product category? [12 marks]
   (b) What action do they have to take with their product portfolio and why? [13 marks]

## Data response question

Using the information in this chapter, answer the following questions.

1. Distinguish the product levels for Dove Soap. [4 marks]
2. Illustrate the likely product portfolio for Unilever, and discuss the product line decisions they have taken. [6 marks]
3. Why are 'power brands' so important to Unilever? [15 marks]

## Chapter Six

# Price

*'In the market economy the price that is offered is counted upon to produce the result that is sought.'*
JK Galbraith, in *The Ultimate Book of Business Quotations,*
S. Cranier, Capstore, 1999

Definition: Price is anything that is charged for a product and comes in many forms, for example rent, tuition fees, rates, commission, wages, and income tax.

## Price determination
Setting the price will depend on the marketing strategy and market forces. When the price is right the producer will find their marketing strategy optimized; for example, in maximising profit and defeating competition.

## Market forces
The **market forces** of supply and demand determine the quantity of goods and services bought and sold and the price at which such transactions take place. As a result marketing decisions have to take into account constant changes in market forces that encourage regular price changes.

For normal products the lower the price the more will be demanded as illustrated by the demand curve (D) in Figure 19, assuming everything else is held constant (known as ceteris paribus). For suppliers in the market it is usually assumed that they will always seek to maximize their sales revenue, so at higher prices they will want to supply more, ceteris paribus, as illustrated by the supply curve (S) in Figure 19.

In Figure 19 the equilibrium price (Pe) and quantity sold (Qe) are established. At this price level the quantity sold times the price per unit sold is the total sales revenue. If the price is set below Pe a shortage will exist, and if set above a surplus will exist. Ideally market forces will clear these surpluses or shortages and restore the equilibrium price (Pe). However this model assumes that the price mechanism is perfect and no imperfections exist such as a lack of information.

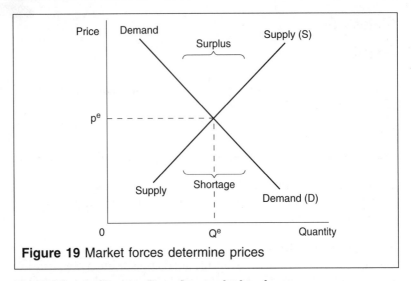

**Figure 19** Market forces determine prices

## Non-price influences on buyer behaviour

Apart from price, changes in 'other factors' determining buyers' behaviour will shift the demand for the product at any price level, as illustrated in Figure 20. Factors causing an increase in demand, as illustrated by a shift outwards in demand from $D^0$ to $D^1$, will lead to market forces pushing the price upwards from $P^0$ to $P^1$, ceteris paribus. Whereas factors causing a shift inwards in demand from $D^0$ to $D^2$, will result in market forces pushing prices downward from $P^0$

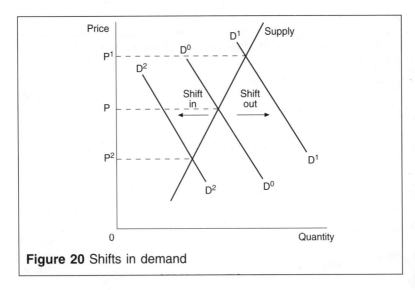

**Figure 20** Shifts in demand

to $P^2$. A successful marketing response will be to anticipate these changes in buyer behaviour. An unsuccessful marketing response might be to resist, like King Canute, the tide of changes in consumer behaviour.

For normal goods an increase in income will increase demand at whatever price. For example, Switzerland is one of the most expensive countries in Europe due to the high disposable incomes of the Swiss pushing up prices by increasing demand for different products.

In terms of the marketing mix a successful advertising campaign will raise demand by ideally changing consumers tastes and preferences in favour of the advertised product.

The price of competitive goods, also known as substitutes, will influence the demand for a product. A rival firm that is price undercutting will reduce demand for the product.

The price of complements, joint demand products, will also affect the demand for the product. In the case of car usage, an increase in the price of petrol may reduce demand for car travel.

Finally future price expectations will also effect the demand for the product. If people expect the price of game consoles such as Nintendo, Sony and Sega to fall they will defer consumption.

## Non-price determinants of supplier behaviour

If more firms enter a market the supply curve will shift outwards from S to $S^1$ resulting in the equilibrium price level decreasing from P to $P^1$, as illustrated in Figure 21.

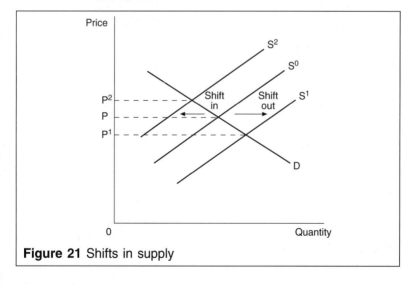

**Figure 21** Shifts in supply

Supply will shift inwards, from S to $S^2$ as illustrated in Figure 21, following an increase in the cost of marketing, distribution or marketing, resulting in an increase in the equilibrium price from P to $P^2$. Changes in exchange rates, inflation, interest rates, regulations, taxes and subsidies will also discourage or encourage the quantity supplied; bringing about price changes beyond the control of the firm..

Finally the objectives of the firms will affect their supply. The firms objective to make a short-term or long-term profit will influence how much they supply and at what price they sell it at.

## Price elasticity of demand

The ability of a firm to pass on to the consumer increased costs of production or taxes by increasing prices, or to keep prices the same and absorb the costs, will depend on their **price elasticity of demand**. The 'price elasticity of demand' for a product measures the responsiveness of its demand to a change in price, as calculated by the percentage change in the quantity demanded by the percentage change in price. If this calculation comes to less than one then demand is said to be 'price inelastic', if it is greater than one it is 'price elastic' and if it is equal to one then demand is 'unit elastic.'

If firms are successful in their marketing campaign in creating brand loyalty then they will find that demand for their product is 'price-inelastic', as illustrated in Figure 22. This means that an increase in

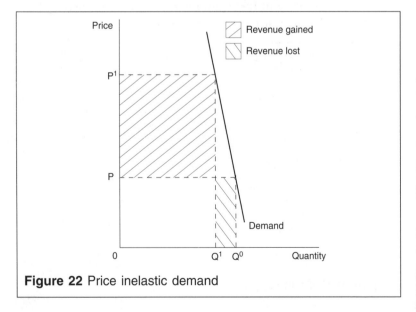

**Figure 22** Price inelastic demand

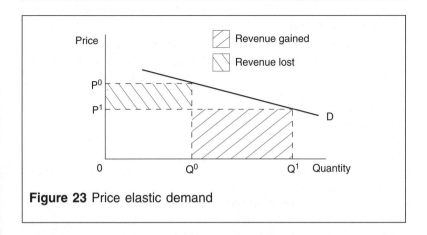

**Figure 23** Price elastic demand

price (P to $P^1$) would result in a smaller percentage drop in demand (Q to $Q^1$), and therefore an increase in sales revenue (unit price times quantity sold). A price cut would lead them to lose sales revenue thus encouraging them to keep their prices artificially high. However in cases when firms keep prices artificially high, the Competition Commission might restrict them for abusing monopolistic power. Price inelasticity also often occurs when a lack of information, inertia or habit means consumers will stick to the product they know.

In a competitive market firms will face a '*price-elastic*' demand curve, as illustrated in Figure 23. A small change in price will now lead to a large change in demand. Hence a price rise might see a collapse in demand whereas a price cut ($P^0$ to $P^1$) might lead to a substantial increase quantity sold ($Q^0$ to $Q^1$) and therefore in total sales revenue.

The percentage of disposable income spent on the product will also affect the price elasticity. In the case of products which take up a small part of disposable income price changes will have little affect on the level of demand, whilst items that take up a larger percentage of disposable income might be more price elastic.

## Income elasticity of demand

The response of demand to changes in income is known as the **income elasticity of demand**. For a normal good this would be calculated as a positive relationship since an increase in income will result in an increase in demand. For an inferior product, like a tape player, there would be a percentage drop in demand as a result of an increase in income.

## Cost-plus pricing

Cost plus pricing, also known as mark-up pricing, concerns setting a price that covers cost plus a mark up for profit. The most common forms of mark up pricing decisions are a mark up as a percentage of cost; or a mark up as a percentage of retail prices. In the case of a CD bought by a shop for £8 and sold for £12 the mark up as a percentage of cost (4 divided by 8 times 100) is 50 percent. Often a mark up is passed down the distribution line. So the manufacturers mark up is passed on to the wholesaler who passes their mark up on to the retailer who adds their own final mark up which is passed onto the consumer.

The *total costs*, which a mark up is based on, are *variable costs* plus fixed costs. Variable costs are the costs associated per unit sold or per customer, and therefore include raw materials, components, energy, distribution and warehousing when storing each unit. Variable costs are *direct costs* because they are charged directly to the unit produced; however not all direct costs are variable costs. *Fixed costs* are the costs associated with production no matter how many units are sold or customers served. Fixed costs are mostly *indirect costs*, known as *overheads*, which are associated with running the business in terms of administration costs, paying salaries, and marketing.

## Absorption pricing

Absorption pricing involves the total costs and a mark up for profit being absorbed into the selling price. Accountants favour absorption pricing as it attempts to cover total costs by sharing them out amongst those units used to manufacture the product. Each unit must therefore absorb its fair share of the total costs. Its advantage is that it ensures that prices are set after all costs have been considered. Its disadvantage is that it assumes that all costs can be accurately estimated and that predictions for demand and output are accurate.

## Contribution pricing

Because of uncertainties in any market, few firms are able to operate a fixed selling price on a cost-plus basis and require a degree of flexibility. This is when contribution pricing is used as a short-term tool. Contribution pricing means that the price is set to at least cover the variable costs and makes a contribution to paying off the total fixed cost. Firms will need to break even in the long run, so contributory pricing will only be successful in the long-term if it succeeds in increasing sales. Contribution pricing might lead to price discrimination or use of loss leaders, and will require the willingness to accept additional customers at cut prices.

## Profit maximising

It is normally assumed that most firms will set their prices at a level of output where they can maximize their profit. Profit maximization (Qm) occurs when the difference between total revenue (TR) and total cost (TC) is greatest.

## Productive efficiency

Alternatively, firms might decide to price at a level of output where they are productively efficient, thereby placing them at a competitive advantage. New firms entering the market will at first experience high start up costs for example buying new machinery and low quantities of variable costs. As they start to expand they will start to benefit from being able to buy in supplies and materials in bulk as well as finances and marketing costs will come down. Firms will also gain from the *experience curve*, a decline in costs as a function of cumulative experience. By driving for market share and moving rapidly down the experience curve, a firm can reap a cost advantage and dominate its industry. These factors mean that average costs come down. Lower average costs resulting from higher output are known as Economies of Scale. Eventually though diseconomies in the form of higher average costs will settle in due to over-staffing and bureaucracy. This is why some firms in the eighties downsized by reducing their scale of production to cut costs and therefore allow a cut in prices.

## Pricing strategies

As a key ingredient in the marketing mix pricing offers an opportunity to meet the marketing strategy. The marketing objectives of entering new markets, surviving or boosting sales will also affect pricing. Price will tend to increase with increased branding, exclusive distribution to a few outlets, and specialising to differentiate the product. The pricing strategy can not be operated in isolation of market forces and its appropriateness to the external environment. For example, premium pricing to make a good seem exclusive, might not be appropriate during a recession when few can afford it. Finally the pricing strategy has to be appropriate to the product, a low quality product that is charged at a high price will quickly drown in the market. These different factors shape specific pricing strategies.

## Psychological pricing

A form of **psychological pricing** is **premium pricing**, when consumers perceive that for a higher price they are getting a higher quality product and will therefore demand more. This applies to attending an exclusive conference, which people believe is likely to have better speakers and clientele to network with because of the higher price. Premium pricing is also used for emergency services as in the case of plumbers.

An alternative psychological strategy is to get the consumer to perceive that the product is under-priced, by stressing price-cuts or 'bargains'. This can be done by using *reference prices*, referring to time specific mark-downs, such as seasonal sales or the past history of the price. *Odd/even pricing* is another a form of psychological pricing as £4.99 is below the £5 price barrier. Lastly *price lining* can be used to meet a range of psychological perceptions, as in the case of CDs being offered at discount prices alongside limited special editions at premium prices.

## Discount pricing and allowances

Discounts are reductions from the normal price and come in different forms. Cash discounts will encourage prompt payment, therefore meeting the objective of having a healthy cash flow. Quantity discounts can be used to encourage people to buy in bulk or be cumulative by offering a rebate for purchases made over time. For example, offering tokens that will add up to a discount will encourage customer loyalty. Allowances are different to discounts in that they are often given to dealers to encourage promotional campaigns. For example, providing free concert tickets and promotional material to encourage a record store to promote an album.

## Promotional pricing

Promotional pricing is used to attract consumers to a store or brand and to build consumer-loyalty. Promotional pricing includes low interest financing, discounts, and loss leaders, which are sold below cost to increase orders for other product. For example, a retailer will place in their shop window a well-known brand as a loss leader, to entice people into the shop.

## Price skimming

This involves firms 'skimming' the profitable cream off the top of the market pricing range, by selling at a high price, as illustrated in Figure 24. It is usually associated with a new product that is launched in a

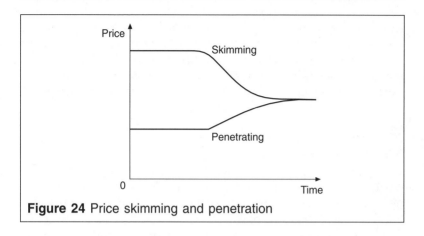

**Figure 24** Price skimming and penetration

luxury or innovative market with little competition and exclusive buyers who want to be the first or few to own the product. **Price skimming** is often justified on the grounds that it rewards firms for research and development. Skimming is a short-term strategy usually to obtain a short-term profit or rectify a short-term cash flow problem. It is usually applied to those products that have a short life cycle, for example fashionable clothing items or computer games. In the long term prices will come down in response to competition or consumer fatigue.

## Penetration pricing
As illustrated in Figure 24, this is diametrically opposite to price skimming as the price is set low to secure a high sales volume, usually because demand is price elastic. The objective is to capture a share of the market quickly by price under-cutting main competitors.

**Penetration pricing** is often used for a new product entering an existing market, by existing firms to defeat competition, and in those industries where large volumes of sales are required to break even. Penetration pricing can take the form of 'limit pricing' when prices are kept low to limit the number of firms entering the market. This is seen as a legitimate form of competition.

**Predatory pricing** is an illegal form of penetrative marketing by seeking to undercut competition to such an extent that they are removed from the market. Once rivals are removed the firm can then increase prices, to make a large profit by establishing itself as a monopoly power in the market. Utility regulators, the Office of Fair-Trading (OFT) and the Competition Commission regulate predatory pricing. To be profitable in the long run, penetrative pricing must lengthen the product life cycle. It can though often trigger retaliation, resulting in a price war as in the case of Walmart buying ASDA and slashing their prices. Penetration pricing uses contribution pricing as the price is set below the total cost and requires spare capacity to exist. Internet companies offer an example of penetrative pricing with lastminute.com offering cut-price flights.

## Discriminatory pricing

**Price discrimination** occurs when different prices are charged for the same good or service. It can only occur when different consumers in separate markets face different price elasticities of demand. For example, British Airways can provide 'economy class' prices to tourists but 'business class' prices to others. Lower prices are charged to 'economy' users because they have a price elastic demand as they can choose when to go on holiday; and 'business' users are charged at a higher price because they have a price inelastic demand, as they have limited choice in getting to their business appointment on time. Other examples would be the location of seats in a theatre or peak and off-peak phone calls. By charging these different prices they can raise their total sales revenue and provide greater service provision. However this will only be possible if the re-sale of the product from one market to another is not possible.

## Product mix pricing strategies

In looking at the product range a strategic view would be to price products across the range, and down product lines.

*Product line pricing* can use price points indicating higher quality as in the case of the star system for hotels. Prices can increase along the line for additional features, as in the case of a car dealer offering additional insurance and air conditioning. This has the added advantage of making the consumer feel that the product is customized, for them by meeting their individual requirements.

*Captive product pricing* occurs by 'locking in' the consumer when they buy the basic product into buying accessories for that product instead of rivals. For example, someone owning a Playstation 2 games console will only be able to buy Playstation games, which can be charged at a premium price as the consumer is unlikely to own a Dreamcast and Dolphin. Another version of captive pricing is *two-part pricing*. This is often used with services offering a fixed fee for the product and then charging variable usage rates, as with mobile phones.

Finally *product bundle* pricing combines a number of options at one price. It has the advantage over product line pricing by reducing uncertainty, and is often offered at a discount price as in the case of package holidays.

## Price changes

Often firms follow the price changes of a main competitor. The reason for this is that not doing so risks taking up a product leader responsibility, which can expose a product to more intense competition. By following price changes in the market, firms are deciding to compete on the grounds of non-price factors such as product improvement, service delivery, promotion and placing the product in the market.

---

### KEY WORDS

| | |
|---|---|
| Market forces | Psychological pricing |
| Price elasticity of demand | Premium pricing |
| Income elasticity of demand | Price skimming |
| Cost plus pricing | Penetration pricing |
| Absorption pricing | Predatory pricing |
| Contribution pricing | Price discrimination |

---

## Further reading

Blois, K., Chapter 10 in *Oxford Textbook of Marketing*, Oxford University Press, 2000.

Brassington, F. and Pettitt, S., Chapter10 and 11 in *Principles of Marketing*, Pearson, 1997.

Davidson, H., Chapter 14 in *Even More Offensive Marketing*, Penguin Books, 1997.

Dibb, S. et al., Part VI in *Marketing*, Houghton & Mifflin, 1997.

## Useful websites

Business education resources: www.bized.ac.uk/.

Competition commission: www.competition-commission.gov.uk

## Essay topics

1. (a) Explain the main factors that influence price setting. [10 marks]
   (b) How can market forces knock a firm off its pricing strategy? [15 marks]

2. (a) Distinguish between market and cost factors behind price deter-
       mination. [15 marks]
   (b) Discuss two pricing strategies widely used by marketing man-
       agers. [10 marks]

## Data response question

### Times accused of predatory pricing

Evidence was submitted to the OFT in 1998 that *The Times* was deliberately
being sold at a loss to eat substantially into newspaper sales of the
Independent and other papers, as shown in Figure 28.

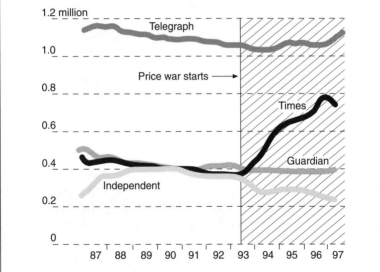

Figure adapted from C Barrie, 'Times defends predatory pricing', *Guardian*,
11 February 1998, p8

**Figure 25** The circulation war

1. What type of pricing strategy is *The Times* being accused of, and
   why is the OFT investigating this? [5 marks]
2. What are the dangers for *The Times* of adopting such a strategy?
   What alternative pricing strategies might it consider? [10marks]
3. How is *The Times* influencing buyer behaviour, and the price it
   can charge in the long run? [10 marks]

*Chapter Seven*

# Place

*'Advertising says to people Here's what we've got. Here's what it
will do for you. Here's how to get it.'*
Leo Burnett

## Place defined
The placing of a product in the market follows the channel of distribution as the ownership of a product passes from manufacturers
to the consumer.

Distribution is an essential ingredient of the marketing mix.
Research has found that, on average 'successful grocery brands
attained 67 per cent distribution in multiple retailers, compared to
17 per cent for unsuccessful launches.' ('Secrets of brand success',
*Marketing*, 26 August 1999)

## Channel marketing
**Channel marketing** concerns the use of horizontal or vertical **distribution channels** that connect the producer to the consumer to distribute products over a distance whilst adding value. Horizontal
distribution channels occur when both firms operate at the same level
in the case of a franchisee and franchiser. Vertical distribution channels, which are more common, operate direct from the manufacturer
to the consumer or via intermediaries (middlemen) to the consumer.
A conventional form of a vertical distribution channel, for convenience goods, is illustrated in Figure 26.

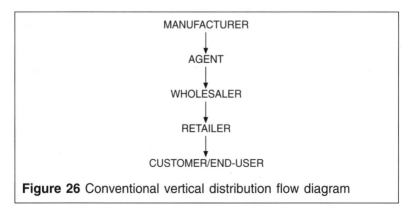

**Figure 26** Conventional vertical distribution flow diagram

## Designing and choosing the distribution channel

In choosing the most appropriate, cost effective and efficient distribution a number of factors need to be considered:

- Maximising customer satisfaction in terms of delivery time, convenience and services expected. The type of product will restrain the distribution channel especially if it is fragile, perishable, or bulky. The flexibility of the channel to changes in marketing, will also be important to firms over the long term.
- Changes in the external environment (PEST) will also help shape the distribution channel: *political* changes in Government and world trade regulations will affect the opening or closing of distribution channels. For example, China becoming a member of the World Trade Organization opened distribution channels into the country. The Single European Market established in 1992 has opened distribution channels across Europe with state support for new road and rail networks, including a second Channel Tunnel.

  *Economic* forces will influence the cost of channel and the revenue that it will reap. An inflationary economy may make a distribution channel more expensive.

  *Social* changes will affect the distribution channel, most notably changes in work-life patterns with fewer women at home during the day to meet door-to-door sales people; and more people working at different times of the day resulting in 24-hour shopping.

  *Technological* changes will lead to closer integration of the manufacturer, intermediary and retailer by using on-line systems that automate dispatch of stock and invoices using **EPOS** (Electronic Point of Sale) data to facilitate rapid response. Also the Internet has increased home shopping.

- The distribution channel will also depend on the type of market. If the market is *exclusive*, selling speciality or prestige goods, then normally consumers will have to travel a distance to obtain these products. The distribution channel will therefore require investing in a sales force operating from a limited number of outlets to enhance image and mark ups. If the market is *selective*, selling shopping or technical products, they will need help from intermediaries distributing the products to geographically dispersed outlets. As they are distributed at point of sale a strong pre and post sales service relationship is important. An *extensive* market, selling convenience goods, will require widespread distribution coverage to reach most outlets. To achieve mass appeal and penetration, especially in foreign markets, will require a long chain of distribution, which can be expensive.

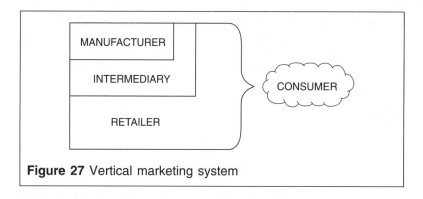

**Figure 27** Vertical marketing system

## Marketing systems

**Vertical marketing systems (VMS)** integrate the manufacturing, intermediaries and retailers into one unit that serves the customer, as illustrated in Figure 27. They are used to avoid channel conflict, when different agents along the channel have different goals and objectives and may often disagree with others along the chain, causing conflict and inefficiency.

There are three types of VMSs: Corporate VMS which involves single ownership of all stages; contractual VMSs in which independent firms at different levels are tied together by contacts for example a franchise or co-operative; and administered VMSs which co-ordinates the stages via the size and power of one of the parties. Increasingly distribution channels have had 'channel captains,' which control other members. Often it is retailers that are dominating the channel by taking over the role of manufacturers and intermediaries, as in the case of Sainsbury. The sheer size of retailers compared to manufacturers places them in a powerful position, as in the case of Wal-Mart with sales of $106bn in 1996 compared to Unilever's sales of just over $50bn.The result of this is that current trends are towards shortening the chain of distribution, missing out the 'middle-man'.

**Horizontal marketing systems** occur when two companies join together for new marketing opportunities. The companies might be competitors or non-competitors, and the relationship might be permanent or temporary. By sharing one distribution channel they can achieve economies of scale.

**Multi-channel marketing systems** occur because it is unusual for a product to be distributed using one channel alone. Usually different channels will be used to reach different consumers, in different market segments. By using a variety of outlets firms can hedge their bets by maximising their chances of reaching the consumer. The danger is that **channel conflict** might emerge. For example a retailer, that had been accepting products to sell to consumers, might be upset and no longer co-operate if their sales are being affected, because the manufacturer is also selling the same product directly to the consumer over the Internet.

## Intermediaries

Whilst there has been talk recently of the demise of 'middle-men', **intermediaries** have benefits by adding value to a product in three ways. Firstly they add *transactional value*, as intermediaries bear the risk of selling the product instead of the manufacturer.

Secondly they add *logistical value* as they can transport, sort and search for a range of products saving the retailer time finding what they need for their target market. Without an intermediary logistically more transactions would have to take place. As shown in Figure 28, without an intermediary nine separate transactions would have to take place instead of six, therefore efficiency is increased.

Thirdly intermediaries have a *facilitating value* since the manufacturer gains by getting cash for their products sold on to the intermediary, without worrying about sales and marketing to the final user or customer. The retailer gains by obtaining credit facilities from

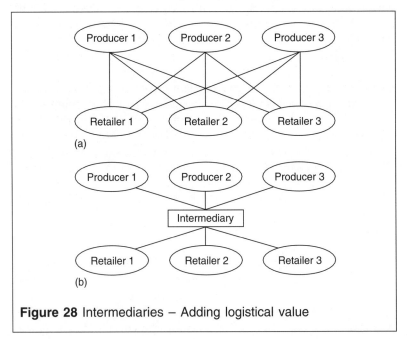

**Figure 28** Intermediaries – Adding logistical value

the wholesaler as well as training, demos, market research, and after sales service.

## Types of intermediaries

The main types of intermediaries are wholesalers, agents, distributors and franchises. **Wholesalers** tend to break bulk by buying bulk from a large manufacturer and breaking it into smaller quantities for retailers. *Agents and Brokers* don't take over ownership of the product, but represent and try to gain sales often for a commission. They are often used to enter foreign markets. An agent will build up a long-term rapport with customers, whereas a broker will be used as a one-off, on a temporary basis or when a special deal is needed. *Distributors and Dealers* increase the accessibility of the product to the market and sometimes provide add on services. For example, in the case of a car showroom, by providing credit, and after sales service support. Finally *franchises* supply and market a product to the specifications of a franchiser, like McDonald's or Body Shop. They increase direct sales because they provide more outlets for the product. By adding value some intermediaries act as Value Added Re-Sellers (**VARS**).

---

### Amazon: real world distribution

NICK PATON WALSH

There is no better place to see the scale and immaturity of Amazon.co.uk than at its new distribution centre, Marston Gate, a warehouse with a solid, pedestrian design a world away from its voguish website. A 30-minute taxi ride from Milton Keynes train station, it is one of three grey monoliths on a building site just off Junction 13 of the M1. The warehouse is vast – about 250,000 sq ft – and has yet to be filled with items from the old warehouse in Slough. Next door, the JCBs are busy constructing another Amazon.co.uk warehouse twice the size. The current warehouse, however, still lacks a canteen.

In many ways Marston Gate reflects the global operation, Amazon.com. Like the company, it is expanding so fast it can't keep up. Behind the sleek website and hype of e-commerce, there is a drab factory floor of a business, that needs to do such dull things as stack and post books, and even turn profits. Here, the seamlessness of the virtual world comes adrift.

---

Extract from 'Wounded Amazon will reign' *The Observer*, 13 February 2000

## Transport modes

In a globalized economy **transport** is the key to distribution. Decisions on which type of transportation to use need to be based on:

- *Speed* – how quickly the product needs to reach the market.
- *Reliability* – shipping has been vulnerable to piracy, even today in the Indian Ocean.
- *Costs* – transportation in separate markets will have different prices.
- *Nature of the product* – whether it is perishable, fragile, expensive or heavy will influence whether the transport mode is capable of carrying the load and accessible.

There are five main options in deciding on transportation:

1. *Road transport*

   Road transport is the most used form of transporting freight in the UK. It has the advantage of being cheap and fast. In using the large road network firms are able to deliver door-to-door, and in not having to rely on timetables flexibility is guaranteed. Firms can deliver products themselves, or use road haulage companies such as Eddie Stobart Ltd, or couriers using cars or motorbike or bicycles. The European Freight Information Service provides a 'dating agency' for the 425,000 road haulage companies in Europe by trying to prevent empty return loads from long destinations. Increasingly governments across Europe are concerned about the environmental consequences of road congestion, and are encouraging a switch to public transport. As a result road transportation has become increasingly expensive, despite the Single European Market encouraging the free flow of goods and services and new motorway networks across Europe being built.

2. *Rail*

   Rail is the most useful method for carrying bulky items long distances to or from ports and distribution centres. For example, companies have direct freight access to Europe through the European Railfreight terminal at Willesden Junction, London. The advantage in using rail is that firms can use full trainloads making transport across Europe, or the USA or Australia cheaper. Governments are also providing incentives to switch freight from road to rail.

3. *Air*

   Air is the most expensive but fastest way of covering long distances. It is ideal for perishable products, which explains why it is now possible to have groceries throughout the year from across the world. Air congestion and pollution are growing problems, and only light non-bulky items can be carried due to capacity restrictions.

4. *Water*

Water is the most economically viable way of transporting bulky items over long distances. Products are shipped by sea, using appropriate vessels (cargo ships or oil tankers); points of entry (harbours accept deeper vessels than ports); and unloading facilities. Inland water transportation is also relatively cheap but slow using rivers, canals and inland seas. The UK government has invested in improving the Canal network in Britain to carry more freight, and Europe's great rivers are heavily used. For example, over half of the Rhine's transport volume is Dutch freight which is off-loaded from Rotterdam, the world largest port.

5. *Pipelines*

Pipelines are used to carry crude oil, associated products and natural gas over long distances, for example North Sea Oil or across the Ukraine.

The problem for many in transportation is not in choosing between alternative types of transportation but in making the link between transport modes. For example, transporting a product from a ship to a train, to a lorry, to a retail outlet is rarely easy. Governments across Europe are spending more to **integrate transport modes** to ensure that the Single European Market is complete in providing the free flow of products across Europe by. For example, by improving the facilities serving the Channel Tunnel.

## Retailers

Retailers assemble a range of goods and services for a target market, using their strengths to differentiate from the competition. They provide *place utility*, in that they are convenient to find and purchase goods. They provide *time utility* in reducing the time to purchase products. They also provide storage, transportation, advice and information in an appropriate environment.

The retailer's *location* will depend on the market, being near passing trade or a geographic segment. Location will also depend on public transport links and parking spaces. The type of good will affect location. For example, a convenience store will need to be based in a densely populated area; whereas nearness to the supplier will be relevant if the good is bulky. Planning permission from the local authority, or at the highest the national government, will also affect location. Finally the cost and viability of the area in terms of land and labour will be important. In central London, the property price boom has pushed a number of smaller cinemas out of business.

## Types of retailers
Retailers can be categorized into stores and non-store retailing.

## Store retailing
Store retailing can be broken down into nine groupings:

1. *Department stores* are organized into departments offering a wide product range and deep product lines, aiming to provide everything the customer wants including restaurants and hairdressers. Examples include: in the UK John Lewis and Debenham's; in France Printemps and Galeries Lafayette; and in Germany Karstadt.
2. *Supermarkets* are large self-service stores in food, convenience items and other product lines for example Tesco, Safeway, and Iceland.
3. *Hypermarkets* are larger than supermarkets and usually located out of town. Examples include in the UK ASDA owned by the US firm Wallmart; in France Intermarché, and in Germany Tengelmann.
4. *Out of town speciality stores* cover a narrow product range usually in DIY or furniture for example IKEA in Brent, outer London.
5. *Town centre speciality stores* are those which specialize in a particular product like Tandy, Waterstones or Clarks shoes.
6. *Convenience stores* plug a gap in the market between superstores and independent operators, for example petrol station stores or corner-shops.
7. *Discount clubs* operate by members joining and obtaining discounts by buying in bulk for example Makro or CostCo.
8. *Town centre and street markets*, for example Portobello Road in London.
9. *Catalogue show rooms* in which consumer choose products from a catalogue, which are sometimes on display, and are then brought to the consumer from the store room, for example Argos.

## Non-store retailing
Non-store retailing comes in three forms:
1. *In-home selling* includes door-to-door cold calling, telephone sales

and party plans like Tupperware parties.

2. *Direct selling* includes mail order catalogues, adverts in newspapers or magazines; TV shopping channels and use of the Internet.
3. *Vending machines* are placed in public and work places, providing for example drinks, food, postage stamps and condoms.
4. *Tele-shopping* is distant shopping using the telephone, Internet shopping and TV. Tele-shopping has blossomed in recent years with the use of credit cards, personal accounts, encryption and passwords to ensure secure financial transactions.

## Retail store environment

The image and atmosphere of a retail store will depend on the exterior and interior of a retail outlet. The *exterior* will include shop front, window displays, entrance and surrounding area.

The *interior* will include the layout, displays and general atmosphere. The *layout* should ideally lead the shopper to cover the store by placing staples in the far corner, or encouraging the customer to browse using a more open planned layout. Alternatively it might focus the customer on one area, for example a beauty boutique layout in a department store. The store's layout can co-ordinate products by their type to help the customer and in some case illustrate the product line depth of the store, for example magazines available in W H Smith. Powerful brands like Sunny Delight can dictate where and how its products are placed in supermarkets to maximize sales. For example, they insist that the drink is sold from supermarket chillers, when it doesn't have to be, to give the impression of being a health drink.

The *displays* will encourage the customer to explore items. For example, fashions store will use themes like seasons, or the products are set in lifestyle contexts using props or mannequins. The *atmosphere* will need to attract the customers' senses. This can be done using sight with attractive colours; smell with department stores placing perfume counters near entrance to entice the customer; sound using appropriate music; and others factors likes carpeting or room temperature. The atmosphere might also be engineered to attract the type and number of customers; avoiding anti-social elements, or overcrowded or empty stores.

## Customer service

The level of **customer service** is essential in the final stage of the chain of distribution but also can be important between each chain of the distribution channel. High quality cost effective customer service is achieved though a number of methods. Being able to deliver on time with good care given to the condition of goods and service on arrival, including sometimes installation, is important. A wide range of goods and services on offer as well as flexibility in order size, opening hours and payment methods will make the customers feel that they have a choice. Administrative accuracy is also important to customer service. For example, invoicing for a product already paid for would cause the customer distress. Equally the reputation for customer service will be enhanced by the ease of dealing with replacements, guarantees and warranties, and the efficient handling of complaints.

---

### KEY WORDS

| | |
|---|---|
| Channel marketing | Intermediaries |
| Distribution channels | VARS |
| EPOS | Wholesalers |
| Vertical marketing systems (VMS) | Transport modes |
| Horizontal marketing systems | Store retailing |
| Multi-channel marketing systems | Customer service |
| Channel conflict | |

---

## Further reading

Brassington, F. and Pettitt, S., Chapter 12 in *Principles of Marketing*, Pearson, 1997.

Danks, S. *et al*, Chapter 11 in *Business Studies*, Letts, 1999.

Davidson, H., Chapters 15 in Even More Offensive Marketing, Penguin Books, 1997.

Dibb, S. *et al*, Part IV in *Marketing*, Houghton & Mifflin, 1997.

## Useful websites

Research library on marketing in the UK including case studies on Sony, British Airways, Unilever, McDonald's: www.marketingcouncil.org

Everything about marketing: Http:marketing.about.com

## Essay topics

1. (a) For a PC firm identify the different types of channels of distribution that are available. [5 marks]

   (b) What are the advantages and disadvantages of using each channel. [10 marks] (c) Discuss the problems of channel conflict that might arise within these channels. [10 marks]

2. (a) What are the different methods of transportation available to distributors. [5 marks]
   (b) Discuss how might they fit into the objective of The Body Shop. [20 marks]

## Data response question

Read the extract below from 'PC war hits the high street' which appeared in the *Guardian* on 10 April 2000 and then answer the questions that follow.

### John Lewis claims Dixons keeps prices high with exclusive sales of leading brands

Full-scale war broke out between Britain's leading computer retailers yesterday, as the John Lewis Partnership threatened to sue Dixons for allegedly abusing its market position.

With the backing of two large high street chains, Comet and Tempo, the partnership accused Dixons of conniving with big manufacturers of personal computers to restrict choice and keep prices high.

John Lewis is furious that Packard Bell and Compaq are withdrawing their computers from its department stores. The two American manufacturers have said that they only want their products to be sold in British high streets through Dixons and its sister chains – Currys and PC World.

A John Lewis director, Nigel Brotherton, said: 'As major high street retailers we are extremely concerned that exclusive supply arrangements by manufacturers for home PCs threaten to restrict choice in terms of service and competition in respect of price.'

1. Explain the likely distribution channel used in the market discussed in the extract. [4 marks]
2. The OFT had refused to intervene because they included the sale of computers on the internet. What might John Lewis have said makes buying computers in a retail outlet different? [6 marks]
3. Why might distributors want an exclusive deal with Dixons? [7 marks]
4. Discuss how consumers might have been affected by the arrangement between Dixons and the two American manufacturers. [8 marks]

## Chapter Eight

# Promotion campaigns

*'Good advertising does not just circulate information. It penetrates
the public mind with desires and belief.'*
Leo Burnett

## The promotional mix

The **promotional mix** covers the total marketing **communication** programme including:

- channel marketing, mainly using advertising on TV, radio, posters,
  in cinemas, newspapers and on the Internet;
- sales promotions, which are usually short-term incentives to
  encourage purchase for example BOGOF (Buy One Get One Free);
- public relations, building up the corporate image and good relations with different publics, for example, issuing a press release;
- direct marketing, using a wide range of methods including direct
  mail shots, tele-marketing, sales representatives, trade shows and
  exhibitions
- sponsorship, for example Ericsson sponsoring the Queens Park
  Rangers football kit.

---

### Kellogg's promotional mix

In 1999 Kellogg's, the worlds leading producer of ready-to-eat cereals,
included an ad push for its Nutri-Grain bars in the UK. Their annual adspend
(year to August 1999, MMS) was:

| | |
|---|---|
| TV | £44,635,709 |
| Press | £2,770,009 |
| Radio | £324,098 |
| Outdoor | £4,451,992 |
| Total | £53,148,460 |

---

These different types of promotion are explored in more detail in
Chapter Nine. This chapter looks at how the promotional mix can
be used overall, by putting together an effective promotional campaign.

## Communication

A successful promotional campaign requires good **communication** skills, to get across the message and objectives of the marketing campaign. Effective communication requires the message to be: received, understood, and accepted. Messages are not always successfully conveyed because of a sender's ineffective use of different promotional materials and how the receiver receives the message. The message may not be clear at the start because the sender of the information is uninteresting, inarticulate, and uncertain or provides too much information. This will continue if the sender fails to check that their message is being understood.

The receivers will not get and act upon the message if they are not motivated to listen, view or read the promotion, or fail to see the importance or relevance of the promotion, or jump too quickly to conclusions about what the promotional message is. Problems will also occur if the receiver is looking or listening out for flaws in the message, especially if they have had a bad experience of the sender before. External barriers to communication will occur is there is a poor environment for example noisy surroundings or trees blocking a billboard. Barriers to communication will prevent the consumer taking action by purchasing the product.

## AIDA model

Promotional activity is about making the consumer aware of the product, and reminding and persuading them to buy the product. It is unlikely that a product will instantaneously create its own demand, known as the weak link theory. Instead it will go through a number of different stages. The most popular of these stage theories is **AIDA** (Strong 1925), meaning awareness, interest, desire and action. Each stage has different objectives and requires different promotional mixes:

- Awareness, occurs when the potential customer is mentally aware that the product exists. Increased product awareness will mostly be achieved using heavy advertising to attract the consumer.
- Interest, is aroused when the consumer seeks more information about the product. This requires less advertising and more personal selling. Product differentiation and improving the image will need to be considered.
- Desire, is created when the consumer wants to buy the product and will search for it. To help this sales promotion techniques and personal selling, by word of mouth, are required. There is less emphasis on advertising than before.

- Action, is stimulated at the point of sale (POS) when the consumer buys the product. Even more sales promotion and personal selling will be required. More emphasis is placed on being flexible in meeting consumer wants. For example, offering different financial options like buying on credit. Minimal advertising is likely to be required now.

These stages will have different time scales for different products and markets, some being almost instantaneous. Feedback is required at each stage since it is unlikely most consumers will move through AIDA as illustrated in Figure 29. In planning a promotional campaign the planner needs to think through and prepare for these stages.

## DAGMAR model
The **DAGMAR** model stands for 'defining advertising goals for measured advertising results'. Like AIDA it measures the effect of advertising in terms of how far the target market has progressed along to taking action by buying the product.

## Planning the promotional campaign
The strategy for a promotional campaign will concern matching the message, format and use of the media, with the marketing objectives, target market and the environment in which the product exists.

In **planning** the promotional campaign it is essential to have clear objectives which might be for the short, medium or long term. It is

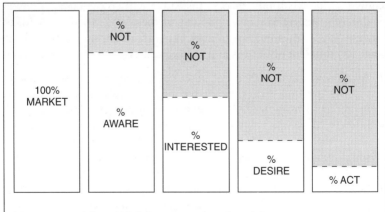

**Figure 29** Using AIDA in promotional activity

also important to get the right promotional mix. For example, a school mini-enterprise would hardly use a national TV campaign.

The *target audience or market* will require different marketing campaigns. The more mass market orientated the product, the greater the need will be for advertising and sales promotion i.e. *channel marketing*, and the less need for *direct* i.e. personal selling. This tends to mean that consumer products will use channel marketing as they often appeal to the mass market, with purchases often made on impulse. Producer products tend to require direct marketing, as they tend to be high valuehigh risk purchases infrequently bought. Consumers will take their time before purchasing producer products, requiring sellers to build up a long-term relationship with the customer. However it is important to remember that to differing degrees most products will use a mix of channel and direct.

## The environment

PEST will influence the planning and implementation of the promotional campaign in different ways:

- Politically laws and regulations will place restrictions on promotional campaigns for example tobacco or alcohol advertising is heavily restricted as indicated in Chapter 9.
- Economically income per head, growth or recession, competition, and unemployment will all play a role.
- Socially changes in work-life patterns, and cultural changes whether generational or increasingly multi-cultural need to be considered.
- Technological developments will provide new opportunities and methods of promotion, as with the Internet

## The influence of push or pull promotional strategies

The promotional mix can take two strategies: **push** or **pull** as illustrated in Figure 30. With a *push strategy* the product is promoted as it is pushed on to the next stage of ownership, which is from the manufacturer to warehouses to retailers to the consumer. With the *pull strategy* the manufacturer outflanks the chain of distribution. This is done by the manufacturer trying to stimulate demand from the consumer, to demand the product from the retailer, who in turn demands it from the wholesaler, who demands it from the manufacturer.

## The influence of the product life cycle

The stage at which the product is at in its *product life cycle* will influ-

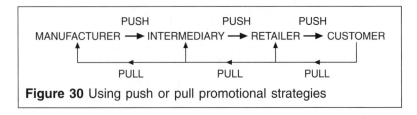

**Figure 30** Using push or pull promotional strategies

ence the promotional campaign. At its introductory stage heavy advertising, sales promotion and personal selling to the retailers to take the new product will be required. During the growth period advertising will need to emphasize how the product is differentiated from others, to increase sales and market share and prepare for maturation. When matured, advertising will be needed to defend and consolidate the product's position in the market. During decline advertising will need to be minimal to remind customers about the product's existence to slow the decline, or advertising support might be completely withdrawn. A re-launch might also be considered, which will require a new promotional campaign with a heavy investment in advertising.

## The influence of the product's position
The position the product is in the market will also influence the promotional campaign requiring different promotional mixes. For example, Stella Artois and Ralph Lauren position themselves as 'aspirational brands' which appeal as quality products that flatter their consumers.

## Budgeting
*'I avoid clients for whom advertising is only a marginal factor in their marketing mix. They have an awkward tendency to raid their advertising appropriations whenever they need cash for other purposes.'* – David Olgilvy, Confessions of an Advertising Man, 1971, Ballantine Books, p.42.

The promotional campaign needs to make an effective and efficient use of the available resources. There are different approaches to budgeting which can be taken that can be broken down to judgmental or data-based.

**Judgmental budget** setting involves guesswork, which can be arbitrary, affordable, or based on the percentage of current or forecast sales. An *arbitrary* based approach will depend on past sales or in the case of a new product launch what it is expected to cost compared to other product launches. An *affordable* approach will look at what money is left after making the product to promote it, which runs the risk of over or under-spending. Basing the budget as a percentage *of current sales*, which are usually the result of the last promotional campaign, can end up either in a virtuous or vicious cycle, with promotional expenditure spiralling upwards or downwards. Finally basing the budget as a *percentage of forecast sales*, whilst similar to past sales, with a future target it is more likely to become self-fulfilling given the promotional expenditure associated with it.

**Data based budget** *setting* is based more on information gathered than guesswork and can be based on competitive parity or objective and task method. *Competitive parity* involves spending the same or more than rivals. However offering a competitive parity approach can lead to competitors retaliating resulting in a price wars or only improving the quality of the promotional campaign rather than the quantity of products sold. The *objective and task method* is seen as the most logical since it matches expenditure to the objectives and tasks required for the promotional strategy. This takes into account considerations like the position in the product life cycle.

Budgets are rarely fixed and flexibility is required in budgeting the promotional campaign to deal with competition, opportunities or emergencies as in the case of the BSE 'Mad Cow' crisis which affected British Beef. This often means that a budget must have a *contingency*, a sum put aside to deal with opportunities or emergencies.

## Implementing the promotional campaign

The promotional campaign might be implemented in one burst, a number of bursts or using a drip-drip effect where by a steady level of promotional activity occurs as illustrated in Figure 31.

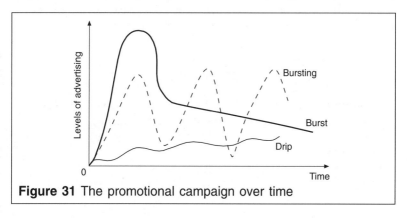

**Figure 31** The promotional campaign over time

## Evaluating the promotion campaign

A promotional campaign must plan for *feedback*, about how the campaign is going or how it went. This should consider what changes it can make, what are its success criteria, and how information can be gathered. This means that any promotional campaign is constantly evolving, and plays a wider role as part of the overall marketing mix.

Different techniques can be used in **evaluating** a campaign. *Aided or prompted recall* methods can be used by, for example, showing a TV commercial and getting respondents to use a monitor indicating favourability, feelings, and how believable or informative they find it. An *unaided or spontaneous **recall*** approach will ask respondents similar questions about adverts seen recently. *Attitude tests*, will ask questions before and after promotional activity to see if change in attitude to the product. *Enquiry tests* track requests for more information about the product, for example the follow up on free-phone enquiries or sales visits. Finally sales tests can be used to gather information on how much is sold in the area where the promotion was undertaken compared to an area where it was not used.

In *evaluating the success* of advertising different targets can be set and measured. The *reach* of the advert will measure the percentage of the target market exposed to the advert at least once. Its *frequency* will cover the number of times households are exposed to the advert over a period of time. The *ratings* an advert receives will depend on the medium: viewing figures for a TV commercial; listening for radio; readership for newspapers or magazines; or number of hits on a Website. The actual *impact* of the advert will rely on a qualitative value of the message exposure via a given medium. For example, 'opportunities to see' (OTS) will measure how many opportunities the target audience has to view or listen to the advert. Evaluation will also use a wide range of methods and will take place during the development of the advert to see how people will respond to it.

---

### KEY WORDS

| | |
|---|---|
| Promotional mix | Push/pull promotional strategies |
| Communication | Judgmental budgeting |
| AIDA | Data based budgeting |
| DAGMAR | Evaluating |
| Planning | Recall tests |

---

## Further reading

Blois, K., Chapter 12 in *The Oxford Textbook of Marketing*, Oxford University Press, 2000.

Brassington, F. and Pettitt, S., Chapter15 in *Principles of Marketing*, Pearson, 1997.

Davidson, H., Chapter 12 in *Even More Offensive Marketing*, Penguin Books, 1997.

Dibb, S. et al., Part V in *Marketing*, Houghton & Mifflin, 1997.

## Useful websites

The Advertising Association: www.adassoc.org.uk
The Direct Marketing Association: www.the-dma.org/

## Essay topics

1. (a) Define 'advertising' and distinguish it from 'promotion'. [10 marks]
   (b) Explain the role of AIDA and DAGMAR models in promotional activity. [15 marks]
2. 'Promotional activity is money well spent'. Discuss in terms of:
   (a) planning [6 marks]
   (b) budgetting [6 marks]
   (c) implementing [6 marks]
   (d) evaluating the promotional campaign. [7 marks]

## Data response question

This task is based on a question set by AQA in 2000. Read the adapted extract and then answer the following questions.

### Harris tweed turns to America to weave a 'sexy' new image

The ailing Harris Tweed industry is hoping to reverse its decline by wooing leading American designers to make its image 'more sexy' and attract a younger market segment. For many years Harris Tweed producers have been adding value to their products by emphasing the durability of their cloth. The industry now hopes to give tweed a more glamorous image for women.

The average Harris Tweed customer is over 50 and male. A spokesman said: 'We need to target people in the 25–35 age range and get into ladies' fashion wear, particularly in America'.

In spite of suggestions of a product-oriented approach in the past, the industry is to spend £2 million on a marketing campaign. The targeting of new market segments signals a rejection of British designers, and industry executives claim that recapturing the American market is their only chance of increasing market share. The share of the lucrative American market held by Harris Tweed has fallen steadily over recent years.

Critics argue that further decline is inevitable. Many believe that there is not enough demand for cloth to justify the proposed level of investment in marketing and that this decision fails to recognise the needs of the market itself. The number of weavers making Harris Tweed has dropped from 400 to 150 over recent years.

*Source:* adapted from *The Daily Telegraph*, 26 January 1998

1. Define the term 'adding value' [2 marks]
2. Explain the benefits that Harris Tweed producers may have gained by selling to a clearly defined market segment. [6 marks]
3. Analyse the possible implications for Harris Tweed producers of a market share which has 'fallen steadily over the years' [8marks]
4. Discuss the factors which might determine the degree of success of a marketing campaign. [9 marks]

## Chapter Nine

# Promotional methods

*'Half the money I spend on advertising is wasted, and the trouble is I don't know which half.'*
Viscount Leverhulme

## Advertising and the media

**Advertising** is paid for 'above line' promotional activity using the **media**. The key therefore to an advertising campaign is buying the right media to show the right ad to the right person at the right time. The decision on which medium to use will depend on considering the cost, target market and appropriateness. Most of the time a company will use a range of media to advertise their product. In the case of Sega they spent over £60 million on their European marketing campaign for Dreamcast, the games console. This included a cross-promotional alliance with BskyB using traditional and on-line advertising. The use of the Internet to advertise is explored in Chapter Ten.

In the UK the main media for advertising are the press and television. In the USA radio is an important medium for advertising; whilst in India, where few own TV sets, the cinema is more important. Across Europe advertising varies, with greater expenditure in Germany followed by the UK, France, Italy and Spain, where incomes are higher and competition is more intense.

In the UK comprehensive up to date sources and costs of advertising are contained in 'British Rates and Data (**BRAD**) – the monthly guide to advertising media', available in most local libraries.

## Television

Using Television has the advantage of being intrusive and ideal for mass marketing. Since 1955 TV advertising in the UK has left memorable adverts with images, jingles and slogans like 'The future's bright, the future's Orange'. When Nick Kamen stripped off his retro 50s style Levi 501 jeans in 1985, to Marvin Gaye's 'I heard it through the grapevine,' it rocketed Levi's sales by eight hundred percent.

TV advertising also has the advantage of being able to target market segments based on programmes, regions and the time of the day. Germany has Europe's biggest TV market with around 33.1 million

---

## Public says yes to ads on the BBC

EMILY BELL

Following reports last week that Prime Minister Tony Blair backs the idea of advertising on the BBC the results of a new Gallup poll suggest that the same is true of the public at large.

The Pace Report, an annual survey of the British TV market, shows that 44 per cent of the public believe that the BBC should carry advertising in order to either replace or lower the licence fee. This is up by 5 percentage points on the previous year.

Source: *Observer*, 'Media', 26 September 1999

German homes owning a TV. Across Europe, advertising expenditure by TV varies as shown in Table 1.

TV advertising time in the UK is sold using a 'spot' system. A 'spot' can last one minute down to seven seconds, and spots are bunched into commercial 'breaks' between programmes. Each of the different broadcast companies charge different rates for their 'spot' times, usually related to viewing times, viewing figures and the incomes per head of the viewers. A 30 second weekday peak time 'spot' on Scottish Grampian TV would cost around £1,250; whereas a similar spot on

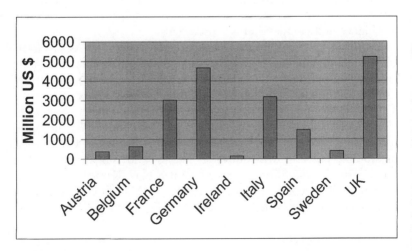

**Table 1** Expenditure on TV advertising in Europe (Source: Euromonitor, 1997)

Carlton TV serving Greater London could cost around £23,000 (Advertising Association, 1998).

A disadvantage with TV advertising is the high wastage caused by those not watching the advert because they are putting the kettle on or otherwise occupied.

'Spot' advertising remains the most common form of advertising on TV in the UK, but other forms of advertising have emerged. Since 1991 programme sponsorship has been allowed. This gives sponsors credit for being associated with a programme in return for a financial contribution, as in the case of Cadbury's sponsorship of Coronation Street, the biggest TV sponsorship deal signed in 1996 for £10 million. Teletext services provide printed information on-screen, advertising air-tickets and other business services. Advertising is also used in Video's, Computer Games and on Inflight Television on planes.

The emergence of Digital Television (DTV) is resulting in a large increase in the number of channels including interactive channels. In March 2000 the UK's first interactive television advertisement was shown. SkyDigital viewers using their remote controllers were able to click on an interactive TV ad for Chicken Tonight's Stir It Up to link to a recipe site and download a product voucher. In marketing terms DTV changes TV content from 'broadcasting' to 'narrowcasting'. Advertisers have to work harder to customize their message and build up a closer relationship with the viewer, as it will be increasingly difficult to target an audience for enough time to convey a message.

## The Press

The advantage with using newspapers and magazines is that they have high coverage, making up the largest group of media in the UK. In Europe advertising expenditure in newspapers and magazines is greatest in Germany, followed by the UK, France, and then Italy and Spain. (Source: Euromonitor, 1997). They also have low production costs compared to TV, can target and have more long-term impact than TV or radio. For example, recipients can cut out and keep adverts or favourable articles. The readership figures of different publications and their buying power will interest advertisers.

Advertising in the press nationally or locally can take two forms. Display adverts can be used, which are larger in size and allow greater flexibility in colour, image, and the position in the newspaper or magazine. Display adverts can also be made to look like news-copy, an **advertorial,** although it has to mention somewhere that it is actually an advertisement.

*'There is no need for advertisements to look like advertisements. If you make them look like editorial pages, you will attract about 50 per cent more readers.'*
– David Ogilvy, *Confessions of an Advertising Man (1971)*, Ballantine Books, p. 108.

Secondly, classified adverts are used, which appear in the classified section and are usually smaller, factual, and black and white.

### National newspapers
The UK has the highest newspaper readership in the world so it provides a useful medium to advertise in. An advert in a national newspaper is quite expensive but still cheaper than TV. For example, a full-page black and white advert in the Sunday Times would cost £57,500 (BRAD April 2000).

*Morning and evening regional, and local newspapers*, can target a local market and are relatively cheap. For example, a full-page black and white advert in the Edinburgh Herald and Post would cost £3,080 (BRAD April 2000).

*Free distribution publications* delivered door to door are paid for through advertisements. Actual readership of the adverts though might be low due to over-exposure of other adverts. However, publications like the Yellow Pages remain the most common means of advertising for businesses.

### Magazines
The cost of a full page colour advert displayed in one edition of a high circulation magazine, like BBC's Radio Times, would be £21,000 (BRAD April 2000). The disadvantage, though, with advertising in magazines is that they usually require long run-in times for copy.

## Radio
The advantage with radio is that it is relatively cheap compared to TV. It allows for greater flexibility, from usual commercial slots to incorporation in a radio programme in the form of sponsorship and competitions. It also has the advantage over TV of greater geographical flexibility with local stations. Today there are over 240 commercial stations in the UK, which are funded from advertising revenue. As on TV, radio adverts are sold as 'spots', with peak listening programmes tending to be in the breakfast and evening rush hour. A 30 second spot on Virgin Radio (AM/National) played Thursday – Friday in rush hour time 1600 – 1900 hours would cost £1,100, compared to a similar spot played Wednesday to Friday on

BRMB (Birmingham) which would cost £700 (Advertising Association '98).

In Europe, advertising expenditure using the radio is illustrated in Table 2.

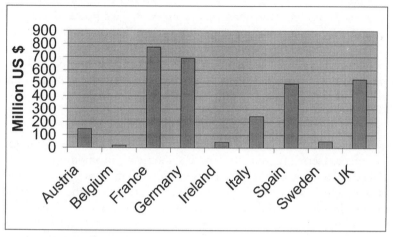

**Table 2** Expenditure on radio advertising in Europe, (Source: Euromonitor,1997)

The disadvantage with radio is that it restricts the advert to the aural medium only and it is difficult to obtain mass-market appeal, even more as the market segments.

## Cinema

Cinema attendance has been on the up in the UK since 1985, but varies across Europe, meaning that it has a greater impact (in descending order) in France, Germany, the UK, Spain and Italy.

The advantage with cinema advertising is that it is intrusive, has a large screen impact, and can be targeted geographically at mostly 15-24 year olds. A 30 second spot played each day for one week in London Cinemas (372 screens) would cost £40,225, compared to £10,035 in Lancashire Cinemas (162 screens) (Advertising Association '98).

The disadvantage with cinema advertising, though, is that it depends on cinema attendance and therefore the popularity of a series of movies. Also cinema adverts can take a long time to produce, and the production process can be expensive.

## Outdoor media

Outdoor media can take various forms from hot air balloons, laser projections to leaflets or point of sale (POS) advertising you might see in a shop; but the most common method remains posters. Posters are highly effective in getting across a simple message, as the Saatchi & Saatchi poster for the Conservative Party did in 1978, paving the way for Margaret Thatcher's victory in 1979. This poster depicted a long queue outside a job centre, with the line 'Labour isn't working.'

Posters can be regional or targeted, for example roadside advertising targeted at car owners. Also the design and sizes of posters can vary from small display notices to roadside hoardings. A national poster campaign using 3,000 sites over four weeks would cost £1,000,000 using roadside hoardings, or £400,000 using bus-shelter size posters (Advertising Association '98).

In Europe advertising expenditure using outdoor media is greatest in France, Germany and then the UK (Source: Euromonitor, 1997)

The advantage with a poster campaign is that, with about 82,000 poster panels nationally, it can reach ninety per cent of the adult mass market in one month. The disadvantage with using posters is that only a simple message can be delivered, which might take time to sink in as the recipient is often passively receiving the message.

## Advertising legal requirements

The advertising 'watchdogs' in the UK are the Advertising Standards Authority (ASA) an independent body whose activities include investigating complaints about most adverts; the ITC (Independent

---

### ASA defends and acts

* Barnado's the children's charity, was justified in using the 'stark image' of a baby injecting heroin to drive home its role as a safe haven, The Advertising Standards Authority said yesterday.

    Rejecting 28 complaints attacking the newspaper campaign as shocking and offensive, the ASA said it was obvious that Barnado's had tried to convey a 'serious and important message'.

* Virgin yesterday withdrew an advert for a video game judged by the ASA to incite violence against pedestrians. The poster for Carmageddon featured a naked bottom with the words 'Pedestrians. Kiss yours goodbye', and underneath: 'Puts the car into carnage' with 'carnage' dripping in red.

    Virgin Interactive Entertainment said the advert was humorous but apologized for the offence caused.

---

Extracts from 'Barnado's drug baby ad justified', The *Guardian*, 5 April 2000

---

## ITC acts

In February 1999 Heat magazine ran a series of advertisements showing people in various situations and locations bursting into flames whilst reading the magazine, including a woman in a bath. Viewers complained that these adverts were 'disturbing', 'shocking' and harmful to those that suffered from fire related incidents. The ITC required the advert to be withdrawn.

The advertising 'Codes' state that: 'All advertisements should be *legal, decent, honest and truthful*'.

---

Television Commission), which regulates TV adverts, and the Radio Authority for radio adverts.

The new 'Codes' issued in October 1999, available on the ASA Web site, include guidelines affecting a number of areas in advertising. For example, adverts are only able to make comparisons 'in the interests of vigorous competition and public information.' However *'comparative advertising'* cannot denigrate other businesses by unfairly attacking or discrediting them.

The same laws that affect any other business also affect advertising. These laws are drawn up by Acts of Parliament in the UK, which also implement European Directives from the European Commission. Some of the most important ones are:

- The European Directive on E-commerce (drafted 1999) means that if an on-line trader mistreats consumers in another country, 'proportionate and effective' legal enforcement action will follow.
- EU Directive on the Sale of Goods (1999) – establishes common minimum consumer rights in the European single market for example the right to be refunded or replacement for goods purchased that are found to be faulty. Implemented in the UK, January 2002.
- Competition Act (1998) protects competition and consumers against price fixing or predatory pricing to force out competition.
- EU Distance Selling Directive (1997) – gives legal protection to people who buy goods and services via mail order, telephone sales and e-commerce. Implemented in the UK, June 2000.
- EU Comparative Advertising Directive (1997) permits comparative advertising throughout the European Union on an equal basis. Implemented in the UK, April 2000.
- Sale of Goods Act (Amendment) Act (1994) – goods advertised must meet the description applied to them.

- The Consumer Protection Act (1987) regulates the use of price indicators used including 'bargain offer' and 'reduced price' to ensure that they are genuine reductions.
- Consumer Credit Act (1974) – advertisements for goods sold on credit must include cash price, credit price and true rate of interest.
- The Trade Descriptions Act (1968 and 1972) makes it illegal for anyone in business to apply a false description to any goods or services offered for sale. For example, if a hotel advertises that it has a sea view, it would have to be true.

In 1999 the Government launched its own 'consumer' protection Web site: www.consumer.gov.uk.

## Below the line

Below the line promotional activity involves the direct control of items in a promotion account that do not depend upon the media and are not outsourced to advertising and creative agencies. They normally include:

- public relations
- sponsorship
- exhibitions
- sales promotions
- personal selling, and
- direct marketing.

## Public Relations

The Institute of Public Relations (IPR) *defines* **public relations** as: 'The deliberate, planned and sustained effort to institute and maintain mutual understanding between an organization and its publics.'

Public relations can be external or internal. External relations with the public can be maintained using the Internet, press releases, briefings, exhibitions, conferences, receptions, events like the Annual General Meeting or a football tournament, and open days including factory tours. Product publications are another form of external PR in using the annual report, videos, magazines, brochures, and books about the company or its product. Internal public relations will include corporate communications including house journals to people in the same trade, or staff briefings.

The main advantage with PR is that it is often a cost effective tool in obtaining mass coverage from a credible third party endorsing the product. As Adidas found with the launch of 'Predator', the first performance enhancing football boots. The initial range of Predator was sold out almost exclusively on the back of the Public Relations campaign surrounding the launch.

Good PR involves obtaining public endorsements that help spread news by 'word of mouth', or 'word of mouse' through e-mails. For example people recommending a new film or book to their friends and family, or members of their chat-room on the Net. The difficulty with public relations though is that it is not easy to control what is reported. Frequently what will be reported will be distorted or be bad news about the product, as in the case of the 'BSE Beef crisis' for the meat industry. In these circumstances public relations will be about how to manage such stories and turn them to the advantage of the product.

Getting good coverage in the media is helped by making press releases newsworthy by using celebrity endorsements and special events or stunts. Often a PR campaign will work on the back of an advertising campaign that gets noticed, thereby creating extra free advertising. French Connection's 'FCUK campaign' and Benetton's long history of campaigns from posters of Aids patients to images of Death Row inmates in 2000 have used these shock tactics.

## Sponsorship
**Sponsorship** is the financial or material support by a company for an independent activity not usually linked directly to the company. Usually the company will not gain directly financially from this activity, as they are acting altruistically.

The different types of sponsorship are usually for teams, events and broadcasts. In sponsoring a team like Manchester United for £30 million, Vodafone obtain a total PR package including access and exposure to a wide range of publics for four years.

## Exhibitions, trade shows and conferences
The main advantage with these types of events is usually their ability to capture and absorb the visitor in the product in an enclosed atmosphere with few distractions. In this environment there are greater opportunities for offering an effective presence and networking to achieve future sales. For most firms it offers a way to launch products, provide demonstrations and re-position as a market leader. For smaller businesses these events can offer a cost effective means of achieving this

Major **exhibitions** centres in the UK provide useful venues for these events including the NEC in Birmingham and Earls Court and

Olympia in London. In Europe the annual 'CeBit' show in Hannover comes closest to being a pan European show. With over 600,000 visitors with 6,500 exhibitors from 66 countries, it is the largest business conference in Europe.

## Sales promotion

The Institute of Sales Promotion defines sales promotion as the '*range of marketing techniques designed within a strategic marketing framework to add value to a product.*'

Sales promotion is about promoting the sales of a product often in a shop or retail outlet or near where it is sold. Sales promotion is known as 'below the line promotional activity' as it encourages brand switching by reducing loyalty to rival brands.

There are three types of sales promotion: business, trade and consumer. *Retail consumer promotions* involve pushing products onto consumers, and involve a number of different methods:

- *Money based* offers issue coupons or vouchers via adverts. When the consumer has gathered enough they can receive cash back rebates or discounts off products.
- *Product based* offers provide 'extra free' either in the form of 20% larger, 12 for 10 or BOGOF (Buy One Get One Free).
- *Cross selling* is a product based promotional method, for example when a bank promotes loans, mortgages and insurance in material sent out with statements.
- **Merchandising** provides gifts either free inside or on products, free with proof of a certain number of purchases, or at cost. An example of an at cost offer is the Andrex 'Bean Toy' puppy promotion, where consumers had to mail off for the Bean Toy with payment and proofs of purchases. Merchandising can also involve competitions and instant win promotions, for example winning a car or holiday.
- *Store based* promotions can use point of sale (POS) displays using new technology. Demonstrations and 'hands on trials' are common, for example playing the latest computer game at a store that sells it.

## Evaluating sales promotion

There are many ways similar to advertising to evaluate sales promotion but the key test is whether total sales have increased after the sales promotion is over. If consumers are only changing their timing of the purchase as a result of the promotion, or hopping between different sales promotions, then it will not be a success.

*'The manufacturer who finds himself up the creek is the short-sighted opportunist who siphons off all his advertising dollars for short-term promotions.'*
– David Ogilvy, *Ogilvy on Advertising* (1985), Vintage Books, p. 169.

## Sales Promotion legal requirements

The UK's Sales Promotion Code says 'All sales promotions should be prepared with a sense of responsibility to consumers and to society; they should be conducted equitably, promptly and efficiently and should be seen to deal fairly and honourably with consumers. Promoters should avoid causing unnecessary disappointment.' Like adverts, sales promotions should be 'legal, decent, honest and truthful.'

---

### HOOVER FAILURE

In 1992 Hoover ran one of the most ill-fated promotions of all time. Hoover offered two free flights to the USA to anyone buying a Hoover worth more than £100. The astronomic cost of this promotion meant that Hoover eventually had to be sold as a company.

---

## Personal selling

**Personal selling** is an inter-personal communication tool used in one-to-one situations. It is characterized by the five P's: Preparation, Prospecting, Pre-approach, Presentation and Post-sales support. It usually involves a *'sales representative'* who finds customers, informs and persuades them to purchase the products of the representative's sponsors. The sales representative may also have the responsibility of co-ordinating within their own organizations the logistics to support the sale. For example, installing new equipment or arranging finance for the client. They can also act as a source for primary research on the target market and competitors. There has been talk in recent years of the demise of sales representatives as intermediaries as they can be expensive, whereas instead all personnel can be engaged in personal selling.

The personal selling process might involve cold calling but it is more likely to be based on careful research contacting more 'responsive' consumers. In the case of Prudential the classic image of personal selling being 'the man from the Pru' has been replaced with Pru' Direct; using the telephone and follow up personal visits.

## Direct marketing

**Direct marketing** is about establishing a direct interaction between the seller and customer utilizing any medium to establish a long-term buyer-seller relationship. It is used to tailor messages to groups or individuals to achieve additional sales by an effective use of a database on customers.

## Techniques of Direct marketing

The main types of direct marketing (apart from the Internet, which is discussed in the next chapter) are:

**Direct mail.** This uses letters, catalogues, and samples mailed to potential customers. AoL and Dell computers are the 'Avon ladies' of the computer world, selling direct to customers by dominating the direct mail market. Often regarded as junk mail, direct mail volume in coverage can have a disadvantage in high wastage and a low response rate. Direct mail using the Internet (e-mail) is fast replacing the postbox, and is obtaining a higher response rate.

**Tele-marketing** usually operating from a telephone call centre, to promote the product to the target market. Tele-marketing can be outbound by contacting the customer or inbound when the customer contacts the seller in response to a promotion such as a competition.

### Call centres take centre stage

Most operators in telemarketing work from call centres, which are the biggest employers in the UK. With globalization centralized call centres are increasingly serving multiple foreign markets, and Internet shopping also means that Web-enabled call centres are being used. This is important given that 'between 70% and 90% of consumers never complete transactions on the Web'.

Extract from 'Call centres must adapt their ways' in *Marketing*, 2 December 1999

Outbound telemarketing is becoming increasingly difficult due to the expansion in mobile phones making it increasingly difficult to contact the target market in a low cost manner. Also regulations have been tightened. In Germany outbound telemarketing is banned and in the UK, some cold calls to residents can be stopped.

## Database management

The advantage of direct marketing to target potential customers relies on the quality of their **database management**. However, the more up to date and comprehensive the database is, the more likely it will be expensive and a drain on resources in gathering information.

## Legal requirement for direct marketing

Because direct marketing relies so heavily on gathering information on individuals in the market it must comply with the provisions of the *Data Protection Act 1984*. The 1984 Act covers 'Personal Data' (including names, addresses and personal information) which is processed on a computer. It provides individuals with certain rights including access to the data, and where appropriate to have the data corrected or deleted. The *Data Protection Act of 1998* also established rules for processing personal information and applies to paper records as well as those held on computers. The '98 Act brings into effect the *EU Data Protection Directive* by harmonizing existing laws across Europe and enabling the transfer of personal data between EU countries.

## Using the promotional mix

Advertising is usually used as a first step to mass-market exposure, so in the A-Z of marketing, A is for Advertising. Over time though a company will use less promotional activity via the media and more by word of mouth, thus establishing the brand's image. What sells in the end is the cult of product personality, consider Carling, Starbucks, or McDonald's, for example. Most promotional activity and expenditure follows a chain from advertising raising awareness to direct marketing. Direct marketing then establishes a relationship, maintaining interest and desire, until sales promotion gets the consumer to act.

---

### KEY WORDS

| | |
|---|---|
| Advertising | Merchandising |
| Media | Personal selling |
| BRAD | Direct marketing |
| Advertorial | Direct mail |
| Public relations | Tele-marketing |
| Sponsorship | Database management |
| Exhibitions | Promotional mix |

---

## Further reading

Danks, S. *et al*, Chapter 10 in *Business Studies*, Letts, 1999.

Dibb, S. *et al*, Chapters 17 and 18 in *Marketing*, Houghton & Mifflin, 1997.

Farbey, A.B., *How to Produce Successful Advertising – A Guide to Strategy, Planning and Targeting*, Kogan Page,1998.

Ogilvy, D., *Olgilvy on Advertising*, Prion, 1999.

## Useful websites

The Advertising Standards Authority: www.asa.org.uk/

Marketing directory: http://advertising.utexas.edu/world

## Essay topics

1. (a) Discuss the advantages and disadvantages of using above line promotional activity?. [15 marks]
   (b) What are the main legal restraints on above line promotional activity. [10 marks]
2. (a) 'Rumours concerning the demise of the sales representative have been greatly exaggerated.' Discuss. [15 marks]
   (b) How can Call Centres support or replace the work of Sales reps? [10 marks]

## Data response question

This task is based on a question set by AQA. Read the extract below adapted from Ian Darby's article which appeared in the *Guardian* on 7 January 1999 and then answer the questions that follow.

### Big Mac blunder hits McDonald's

McDonald's is planning to push ahead with a range of other sales promotions to mark its 25th anniversary in the UK despite this week's Big Mac fiasco.

However the burger giant is unlikely to repeat the 'Buy One Big Mac, Get One Free' offer which it launched in December to to cover Christmas 1998 and the New Year. This promotion led to one of the biggest marketing errors in UK history.

McDonald's ran into problems last weekend with some restaurants experiencing eight times the usual demand for Big Macs which sell for £1.99. The 'Two for One' offer meant there was effectively a 50% price cut. Several restaurants were forced to close due to over-crowding and many customers were turned away when Big Macs ran out.

Television advertising was used to promote the offer, but a large number of restaurants found they could not cope. The Independent Television Commission will consider 21 complaints from the public. McDonald's was rapped by the tabloid press, labelled 'Ham Bungler's and 'Silly Burgers'.

The burger chain took full page advertisements in national and regional papers to apologise for the confusion.

1. Why do you think McDonald's used television as a means of advertising this sales promotion? [5 marks]
2. Examine the likely marketing objectives behind the promotions used to celebrate the 25th anniversary of McDonald's in the UK. [6 marks]
3. Calculate the price elasticity of demand for Big Macs if, as a result of the 'Two for One' offer, total sales increased from two million to four million Big Macs. [5 marks]
4. Explain why Macdonald's often use psychological pricing for many of its products, such as charging £1.99 or £2.95. [4 marks]
5. To what extent might the 'Buy One Big Mac, Get One Free' marketing disaster have been a result of poor market research? [10 marks]

*Chapter Ten*

# Development in marketing: relationship, e-commerce and international

*'In the future, marketing has to be about creating value in the minds of the consumers.'*
Sergio Zyman (See Chapter 3, page 28)

## Relationship marketing

**Relationship marketing** focuses on developing a close relationship with your customer. It has been described as: *'The relentless pursuit of an almost familial bond between customer and product.'* (Tom Peters, *The pursuit of Wow! – every person's guide to topsy-turvy times*, 1995, Macmillan).

Relationship marketing has grown in prominence as firms work to retain customers, when faced with increased competition from a globalized market. The lack of flexibility in traditional advertising, and the slowness of it to respond to changes in consumer patterns of behaviour, have meant that the traditional marketing mix has been increasingly unsuccessful. In the traditional market place the focus was on securing the **transaction**. Relationship marketing goes beyond conventional direct marketing or loyalty campaigns by seeking to establish an interactive long-term relationship with targeted existing and potential customers.

In marketing communications the focus in relationship marketing is establishing a dialogue rather than broadcasting about the product. Usually these relationships are long term and mutually beneficial, fulfilling promises made. Marketing has always attracted customers with the promise of what the firm or product can deliver. Relationship marketing sees fulfilling promises as a basis for achieving customer satisfaction and maintaining retention. For example, British Airways cheap flight operator GO succeeds by low expectations being over-fulfilled. The building and maintaining of trust on both sides of the relationship is also important, especially on the Internet, that a good will be delivered and payment received.

In relationship marketing all activities which involve an inter-relationship with the customer become relevant. This requires successful 'internal marketing' ensuring that all employees of the firm are in effect 'part-time' marketers. In doing this the firm creates more value

---

## RELATIONSHIP MARKETING WINNERS OF '99

The winners of the 'Marketing' magazine award in 1999 went to 'Club Carling'. Bass Brewers' relationship marketing programme was designed to recruit 18-34 year olds to Club Carling. Recruitment methods included: pub promotions, direct mailings to 'cold lists', interactive kiosks and 'member-get-member' drives. The main focus of the membership was the Club's quarterly magazine focused on the target audience main interest – girls, football and pubs. The use of the magazine and questionnaires enabled Carling to produce a database to target those who drink competitive brands more to switch to become loyal Carling drinkers.

---

for its customers than the core product itself, thereby allowing for tighter ties to the customer and premium pricing. These tighter ties are secured by the technical know-how or social care. For example, Boots offers in-store consultations with beauticians to both men and women, with a strong emphasis on customer care.

In relationship marketing the product orientated 4 Ps of the marketing mix become a customer – orientated marketing mix known as the 4 Cs:

- *Place* becomes **convenience** to the customer.
- *Price* becomes **cost** to the user, including customer's transportation.
- *Promotion* becomes **communication,** a two way dialogue.
- *Product* becomes **customer values,** needs and wants.

Transaction based marketing might also lose out to relationship marketing by not understanding customer satisfaction. A hard-sell advertising campaign might successfully expand or retain a large market share, but beneath the data there might exist a high turnover of customers dissatisfied with the product being replaced with new customers. With relationship marketing it is possible for a firm to identify individual levels of customer satisfaction, even in a mass market. Safeway used its database from holders of its ABC loyalty card to identify and stop the drift of high spending customers showing signs of defecting to other retailers. By gathering information constantly, on a daily basis from every source of customer contact, a wealth of information can be obtained for decision making.

## Developments in e-commerce

E-commerce, or e-business, concerns the buying and marketing of product using the web-sites and e-mail transactions on the internet. With the rise of **Interactive Electronic Marketing** on the phone (using WAP), television and computers, customers are no longer passive recipients of promotional activity. Instead they are interacting with firms about what products they want and how they wish to acquire them. As a result market research gathered by firms is no longer about the mass market but individuals. Instead of looking at changes with demographic groups and how best to target them, the new demographic unit is one. The ability of the firm to remember individual tastes and preferences is now central to their success. What firms gain from the Internet is economies of attention. In the case of the bookseller BoL.com, this means the longer a customer spends on their Web site the more likely they are to buy their books and stick with BoL (Books on-line) who gain more information on them. To do this they need to build an ongoing relationship with the customer to maintain customer loyalty. As a result, media is changing as a tool of propaganda informing the public into an interactive device to promote inter-relationships.

## Permission marketing

A type of relationship marketing is '**permission marketing**' (Seth Godin, *Permission Marketing*, Simon and Schuster 1999). This has gained prominence as markets have become saturated by messages. In this situation adverts which interrupt peoples lives, eat into their most valuable commodity – time, and as a result they are switching off. Traditional marketing, like a TV commercial breaking into a favourite programme, or a tele-marketing call interrupting the family dinner, is experiencing diminishing returns.

The easy way to cut through the crowd is therefore to get the consumer to give their 'permission' to be marketed to. Volunteering to be marketed to requires the use of incentives like competitions, free samples, or free-phone. Once they have volunteered an opportunity for a long-term relationship, the marketing situation can develop. 'By talking only to volunteers, Permission Marketing guarantees that consumers pay more attention to their marketing message,' says Seth Godin, Yahoo's direct marketing chief. According to Godin permission marketing best works on the internet, as illustrated by

Amazon.co.uk. Instead of just using banner adverts on a web site, firms like Amazon encourage customers to give their permission to interact with the firm using e-mail. For example, Amazon make their site feel like a book club by urging consumers to provide book reviews.

## Mass customization
Product development is accelerating in e-commerce with products being tailored to meet individual customer requirements at blinding speeds. Instead of mass marketing to sell the mass produced products, **mass customization** allows customers needs to be met as individuals. For example with Dell computers consumers specify what they want the computer to do and then Dell build to order.

## Disintermediation
The ability of the internet to establish direct marketing relationships between the manufacturer and customer or end-user has put into question the need for intermediaries, be it the travelling salesman to retail outlets. In the case of Amazon.co.uk they do not have the traditional problems of book stores of having a large stock plus paying high rents, whilst at the same time they can offer every English-language book in print. Further to this, the ability to download software across the Internet can reduce distribution costs to zero. This has been described as the demise of the middleman, or '**disintermediation**'. **Globalization** which has accelerated as a result of light-speed communications, home-shopping, computer-aided designs, and advances in logistics have enabled firms to out-source production and services required. This has meant that the traditional role of manufacturers in the chain of distribution has been radically altered. Not only have manufacturers the ability now to take over the role of intermediaries but also their very manufacturing role can be out-sourced leaving them in effect as purely service-based organizations.

*'Shoemaker Nike makes no shoes; its work is research and development, design, marketing, and distribution—all services.'* (Source: Thomas Stewart 'A New 500 for the Economy,' *Fortune*, 15 May 1995.)

## Cybermediaries
Intermediaries have not completely disappeared though. Instead the powerful intermediaries who are emerging are the transport operators and **cybermediaries**. Transport operators play a key role in meeting service expectations of cheap and quick delivery of physical

products purchased on-line in the global economy. According to Michael Dell, of Dell computers: 'efficiency in execution is at least as important as products and services.' (*Guardian*, Online, September 23, 1999 p. 12). Cybermediaries include companies like Alta-Vista who manage access to information on the net, as a go between for the potential customer and manufacturer's web site.

## On-line advertising

To advertise on the net firms need to ensure that their products are placed in the most popularly used search engines, and web sites. By clicking on a 'Ben and Jerry's Ice Cream' hypertext link, the user is connected through to the Ben and Jerry's Ice Cream web site. Also, when the potential customer has finally got through to their web site, the firm needs to ensure that their site offers the latest inter-activity, to ensure a direct response. Web sites that simply provide a list of local retail outlets are outdated.

| EMERGING TYPES OF ONLINE ADVERTISING | |
|---|---|
| Banners | Static or animated poster-style advertsiements |
| Buttons | Thumbnail graphic hotlink to advertiser site |
| Interjacent third-party | Animated 'comercial break' between display of Web pages |
| Sponsored third-party | Sponsor seeking to associate brand values with Web site |

Source: OXIRM used in J Reynolds, Reaching the virtual customer, Mastering Global Business, Part 7, *Financial Times*, p12.

## Locationless marketing

Instead of relying on locating near the customer, e-commerce is based on service. Marketing is therefore increasingly **locationless** since selling, training and management can be conducted from anywhere with access to the Internet. Products promoted on the Internet also become locationless in that they can be bought anywhere in the world. In the case of software the distribution costs are zero, as the consumer can download the software across the Net. As the importance of place disappears, the ability of firms to connect to individual firms is becoming increasingly important – across geographical, language, and organizational barriers. However, local content on web sites is vital in delivering the perception of being close.

With the increased use of the Internet even the local corner-shop has the opportunity to be a global shop. Those firms which do step into the international market are gaining from developments across the world in market research, design, production, marketing and finance. This means that increasingly international marketing is relevant to all firms.

---

## Invasion of the e-men

JIM McCLELLAN

As far as online retail is concerned, the Americans are coming.

Many of the big names are already here. Both Amazon, the leading online retailer, and eBay, the leading online auction site, have .co.uk operations. They will be joined by the hugely successful toy retail company eToys this autumn [2000].

It's not hard to see why these companies are coming over here. There's the shared language, obviously. And many of these companies' stock values are based in part on business plans with global dimensions. So they need to expand into Europe to keep the markets happy.

The UK net market is becoming increasingly attractive. Thanks to the free Internet service providers (ISPs), 10 million Britons are online and, according to the recent Which? Online survey, they are increasingly interested in net shopping. Some 40% of net users have tried buying online, with 10% describing themselves as regular net shoppers. Those figures will rise soon as the 3 million net users who've come online in the past year try their hand at buying online. (It takes around a year for someone to feel comfortable enough online to move on to shopping.)

Source: Extract from The *Guardian*, 23 September 1999

---

## Developments in international marketing

*'Any communication or marketing professional needs cross-cultural research and communication skills to be able to succeed in the future.'* Marye Tharp (1996), Associate Professor of Advertising, The University of Texas at Austin (www.utexas.edu/coc/adv/research/quotes).

## Globalization

Globalization concerns the convergence of consumer tastes and aspirations around the world, especially in youth culture and amongst the affluent. Whilst foreign trade is centuries old, globalization is a more recent phenomenon, accelerated by booming economies and the collapse of trade barriers.

The pressures from globalization mean brands have adopted global names; in the UK Snickers used to be Marathon and Starburst was known as Opal Fruits. Product standardization is also taking place to crack the European market, as successfully done by Nestle's Nescafe with its heavy reliance on advertising with memorable visual images.

## Eurobrands

In Europe firms have attempted to introduce 'Eurobrands,' which communicate the same brand image across the European market. However given the problem of different cultures, national identities and languages Eurobrands have been stuck between coming across as too bland, being spread too thin and being out-competed by a local brand. Nestlé has sought to overcome the latter by buying local brands across Europe. As the European Union deepens and widens beyond its fifteen member states in 2000 towards 20 covering 500 million people, and the Single European Market develops and competition intensifies, it is clear that Eurobrands will become a permanent feature of the European market. At the same time the global economy mean that global brands might over-take them in the process.

## Foreign market entry

The most straightforward approach to entering foreign markets is to directly export to the country and hope for the best. Often this has taken the form of 'border-hopping' by entering neighbouring countries. In Europe hypermarket companies like Auchan (France) have entered Spain and Portugal whilst Metro (German), Europe's largest hypermarket company, has moved into the Czech Republic, Hungary and Poland as well as fourteen other countries around the world. A more long-term approach is to try to establish the company in the foreign market. This can be difficult given the lack of knowledge of the local market. An alternative method might be to export indirectly, by using intermediaries from within the country being exported to for example a sales agent. Joint ventures will gain entry by trading in knowledge and expertise. For example, by licensing the firm's trade mark or patent for a royalty to a manufacturer in a foreign country to produce the product under the firms own name, in the form of a franchise or contract. Franchises tend to work best when the supplier provides a product not available in the local market as in the case of the Italian clothes company Benetton.

If the enterprise the firm is linking up with is a large business, it might decide to operate under joint ownership forming a strategic alliance by sharing management expertise as in the case of the Euro Air-Bus or Euro-fighter. Acquisition is another method of entry by purchasing another firm, as in the ill-fated case of Germany's BMW and the UK's Rover or working together, or the German Gehe group buying Lloyd's Chemists in the UK, making it the largest domestic chemist chain.

Finally a firm might enter by directly investing in the foreign market by establishing sales subsidiaries or manufacturing subsidiaries with foreign assembly or manufacturing facilities as Nissan did in Sunderland during the 1980s.

---

## TESCO IN EUROPE

Tesco has ventured into the European market using a variety of methods. Its first venture was in 1978 when it acquired stores in Ireland, which were later sold. Then in 1993 it acquired stores in France, but again had to sell them later in 1997 due to planning restrictions. Since then it has focused its energies on Central Europe. In Hungary, Poland, Slovakia and the Czech Republic it has acquired stores and has opened new hypermarkets, often operating under its own name.

---

## Market entry strategies

*Own brand focus* have been used by market leaders in promoting their own brands abroad as in the case of Benetton (Italy), Body Shop (UK), C&A (the Netherlands), Ikea (Sweden), and Zara (Spain) the fast growing fashion store. Most of these firms manufacture, distribute and retail their own brands.

'*Category killers*' are those brands that seek world domination in foreign markets destroying competition by aggressive marketing by offering deep discounts as in the case of Netto (Denmark), and product depth as in the case of Ikea (Sweden) trading in 28 countries.

*Niche retailers* target a small segment of the population for example promoting Pokémon products to children or a narrow product range as in the case of many UK companies like The Body Shop trading in 46 countries, Tie Rack in 30 and HMV in nine.

*Aiming upmarket* by offering excellence, as in the case of Marks and Spencer's entry into Germany, which placed a special emphasis on the German consumers concern for high quality products and customer care.

---

### KEY WORDS

| | |
|---|---|
| Relationship marketing | Disintermediation |
| Transaction marketing | Globalization |
| Interactive electronic marketing | Cybermediaries |
| Permission marketing | Locationless marketing |
| Mass customization | Eurobrands |

---

## Further reading

Jonathan Gabay, J., Page 58 in *Succesful cyberm@rketing in a week*, Hodder & Stoughton, 2000.

S Godin, S., *Permission Marketing*. Simon & Schuster,1999.

Terpstra, V. and Sarathy, R., *International Marketing*, Dryden, 2000.

Zyman, S., Conclusion p. 233 in *The End of Marketing As We Know It*, Harper Collins, 1999.

## Useful websites

Market trends and reports for on-line marketers: www.forrester.com
The European server: www.europa.eu.int/
Export advice: www.tradepartners.gov.uk

## Essay topics

1. Relationship marketing is another term for direct marketing. Discuss. [25 marks]
2. The internet is revolutionizing the world of marketing. Discuss. [25 marks]

## Data response question

Read the article below, which appeared in the Lex column, *Financial Times* on 11 April 2000 and then answer the questions that follow.

## Tesco.com

Good news from Tesco sounds like a broken record. While the rest of UK retailing is having a dismal time, Tesco on Tuesday reported sales growth of 10 per cent and stable margins. Monotonous, maybe, but music to investors' ears: the shares were up another 6 per cent on Tuesday. Over the last five years, Tesco has won the UK supermarket battle by focusing on and winning consumers' trust.

Through Tesco.com – to be put under separate management to help Tesco stay ahead of rivals – it can now attempt to leverage this trust. Groceries over the internet are not that exciting. Using the customer base to sell other products, from books to banking, is far more so. But it looks as though continued UK market leadership and online growth are in the share price already.

The real potential lies in expansion abroad. Tesco may think it can go it alone here, with its divisions in Asia and Eastern Europe. Perhaps. But a merger looks a better proposition and Carrefour looks like the obvious partner. The French group has international scale and maturity while Tesco could contribute its expertise in cutting costs and supply chain management.

1. How might Tesco have applied the use of relationship marketing in the retail sector? [5 marks]
2. What are the consequences of selling 'Groceries over the Internet' for Tesco? [7 marks]
3. For Tesco: 'The real potential lies in expansion abroad.' Discuss. [7 marks]
4. Discuss two ways another supermarket could seek to improve its performance [6 marks]

# Conclusion

The objectives of the book have been to provide a concise account of marketing in the UK and Europe, to emphasize that marketing is about a lot more than selling and advertising, and to discuss current developments in marketing.

At a time of great change marketing is central to how firms and organizations thrive or die. Currently there are doubts about whether the e-commerce bubble of recent years is about to burst. The key marketing test for e-business will be in their ability to deliver on the high expectations that have been set.

Relationship marketing, with its emphasis on the long term, is also facing stiff competition from those able to sell the cheapest. Small companies with small margins are being swallowed up or driven under by the larger world corporations, multinationals.

'Cool Britannia' has been the new brand image for the UK but there are doubts about the ability of UK firms to survive given the strength of the pound and stiffer competition in the EU market. To counter this the UK Government, through the Department for Trade and Industry and the Design Council, is providing assistance to UK firms. Help with marketing is also provided by three key organizations:

- The Chartered Institute of Marketing (CIM) which is Europe's largest professional marketing body.
- The Marketing Society is a leading practitioner for marketers.
- The Marketing Council supports firms to see the importance of a marketing approach to business success.

Marketing has underpinned UK and European firms, individuals and organizations that have been successful in the late nineties and early 'noughties':

- Richard Branson and 'Virgin' as leading world brand names.
- The dominance of Psion and European mobile phones companies by leading innovations in new product development.
- IKEA's dominance of the furniture market by creating a lifestyle around their brand.

Having read this book, you should now be confident that you understand the key marketing terms and can apply marketing analysis to a wide range of firms or situations.

# Index

ABC1 system 7
Above the line 101
Absorption pricing 72
ACORN 8
Advertising 101
AIDA 7, 93
Ansoff Matrix 34
ASA 108–9

Behaviouristic segment 7
Below the line 110
BOGOF 112
Boston box 27
BRAD 101
Branding 59–62
Budget 18, 96
Bundle pricing 78
Buyer behaviour 68

Call centres 115
Category killers 128
Cause related marketing (CRM) 17
Channel marketing 81
Competitive position 23
Competitive postures 36
Concentrated strategy 25
Contribution pricing 72
Cost-plus pricing 72
Customer service 89
Customization 10, 122
Cybermediaries 123

DAGMAR 94
Data protection act 52, 115
Demographic segment 6
Design 58
Differentiated strategy 24–5
Digital TV 103–4

Direct mail 114
Direct Marketing 114
Discounts 75
Disintermediation 122
Disruptive competition 37
Distribution channel 82

E-commerce 121
Environment 12, 20
EPOS 42, 82
Eurobrands 126
Extension strategy 31

FMCGs 5, 29, 60
Focus groups 42–3
Four C's 120
Four Ps 17

GE Matrix 32
Geographic segment 6
Globalization 123, 126

Implementation 17
Innovation 63
Interactive Electronic Marketing 121
Intermediaries 84–5
International marketing 125
ITC 108

Junk mail 114

Legal controls 108–110
Likert scale 43
Locationless marketing 124

Macro strategy 23
Market audit 20
Market challenger 36
Market follower 35

Market forces 67
Market information systems 40
Market leader 35
Market orientated 5
Market research 40
Market segments 6
Market share 15
Marketing cycle 20
Marketing mix 2, 17, 20
Marketing plan 11
Maslow 3
Media 101
Micro marketing 9
Micro strategy 24
Mission statement 12

Niche 9, 36, 128

OFT 77
Outdoor media 107

Packaging 59
Patents 60
Penetrating 76
Permission marketing 121
Personal selling 113
PEST 12, 20, 82, 95
Pester power 7
Place 17, 81
Positioning strategy 25
Predatory pricing 76
Press 104
Price 71, 72
Price discrimination 78
Price elasticity of demand 70
Pricing strategies 74
Primary research 42
Product 17, 54
Product life cycle 23, 29, 63–4, 95
Product mix/portfolio 55
Production orientated 4

Productive efficiency 73
Productivity 20
Profit maximising 73
Profitability 15
Promotion 17, 92
Promotional mix 92
Promotional strategies 95
Psychographic segment 6
Psychological pricing 75
Public relations 110

Qualitative research 49–50
Quantitative research 49–50

Relationship marketing 119
Re-launch 22
Repositioning 25
Retailers 87–9

Sales promotion 112
Sales representative 113
Sampling 44
Secondary research 47
Skimming 76
Socio Economic Groups 7
Spot advertising 103, 106
Standard deviation 47
Statistical analysis 45
Strategic marketing positions 35
Strategic models 27
Strategy 17, 20, 23
Supplier behaviour 69
SWOT 14, 20

Tele-marketing 114
Trade Mark 60
Trade Shows 112
Transport 86–7

Undifferentiated strategy 24
USP 25

VMS 83